ISBN 1-58660-196-2

In the U.S.A. this book is published by Promise
Press, a division of Barbour Publishing, Inc.,
Uhrichsville, Ohio.
All rights reserved.

Scriptures quoted from the *Good News Bible*
published by The Bible Societies/Harper Collins
Publishers Ltd., UK, © American Bible Society,
1966, 1971, 1976, 1992. Used by permission.

Printed in Malaysia.

Me and God

This special book belongs to:

_____

> Place a
> picture of
> yourself
> here

PROMISE PRESS

An Imprint of Barbour Publishing

"I do not call you servants any longer, because a servant does not know what his master is doing. Instead, I call you friends, because I have told you everything I heard from my Father."

John 15:15 GNB

Dear Friend,

Friendship is very important. We all need a friend. . .someone to talk to who cares. Someone to take our troubles to when we need help. Someone to keep us company when we are afraid, who knows the way when we are lost. Someone to share our hopes and dreams, who can rejoice in our highs and comfort us through our lows.

Friends are very special. I love spending time with My friends, don't you? Let's meet every day. . . .

Your biggest, bestest Friend,

Jesus

January 1

A Year's Adventure

 Mark 1:16–18

Wow! A brand-new year to explore together. How exciting! Don't be tempted to worry about what is to come; each day is safe in My hands. And don't be tempted to look back at the mistakes of the past year—that will only hold you back. Let's enjoy this year together. . .what fun! What adventure!

   One step at a time. . .

Pray. . .
Lord, I'm sorry for the mistakes that I have made in the past. Please forgive me, and help me not to make the same mistakes this year.

January 2

Be Prepared

 Galatians 6:9–10

Always be ready to help others we meet along the way on our year-long adventure. We're on a mission to help others, with a smile, an encouraging word, or a helping hand. Are you ready? Let's go!

Pray...
Lord, I want to learn to be more like You and to do the things You do.

January 3

A Safe Future

 Psalm 33:20–22

Jesus loves; Jesus helps; Jesus fights;
Jesus wins! All the good things that I
have planned for you this year
will happen, little by little.
Will you trust and follow Me
this year?

Think...
If you are willing to follow Jesus and to do all He asks, tell Him...

January 4

Don't Rush Off

 Proverbs 4:11

I know that you are eager to get started on the great adventure I have planned for you, but don't be tempted to rush ahead, or you will miss My instructions.

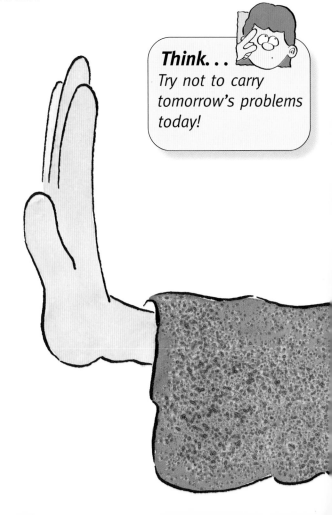

Think...
Try not to carry tomorrow's problems today!

January 5

Pass the Blessing

 Mark 12:41–44

I bless those who bless others: The more you pass on–the more I bless. You may not think that you have much to give, but it's not the *amount* you give but your willingness to giving what you have.

Pray...
Who can I bless today, Lord?

January 6

Love Is the Key

 1 Corinthians 13:4–7

Love finds a way to open up the hardest situations: misunderstandings at school, trouble with a bully or even a friend, difficult brothers or sisters. . .love will find a way.

Pray. . .
Please help me to see people the way You do and to love people with Your love.

January 7

Happy Words

 Proverbs 25:11

The words you speak can make people happy or
sad. I like to speak words that make
people happy, don't you?

Pray...
Lord, please help me
to say the right
things today.

January 8

Love Sometimes Says *"No"*

 Hebrews 12:7–11

Love doesn't always say *"yes."* Sometimes My answer to your prayers may be *"no,"* because I know what is best for you. Trust Me and be happy with My answers–I love you!

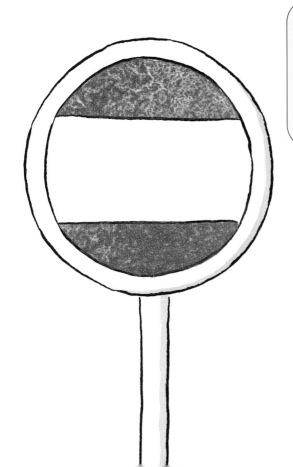

Think. . .
Am I prepared to accept "no" as an answer! Can I trust that Jesus knows best?

January 9

I Know You

 Psalm 139:1–10

No matter what may happen today, stay calm and rest in Me. I know your strengths and your weaknesses, and I won't ask you to do anything that I know you can't do. If you find yourself under pressure, perhaps it is because you are doing something that I haven't asked you to do.

Think. . .
Am I doing something that Jesus hasn't asked me to?

January 10

Time to Stop

 Mark 6:30–32

Stop, look, listen. Some of the things you learn from Me need time to sink in. Take time to stop and think about some of those things before rushing ahead. Start today.

Pray...
Lord, please help me to remember the important things and put them into practice.

January 11

Time to Think

 John 16:13

There may be times when you sit with Me in silence. Don't worry—you are not on your own. I am with you, but before I say something new I want to make sure that you understand what I have already said. Can you remember some of the things I taught you in the past?

Think. . .
What have I learned? What do I know about Jesus and how to follow and please Him?

January 12

Pass It On

 Matthew 28:19–20

Do you find these times together helpful? If so, pass it on. Tell others what you have learned so that they, too, can share in the blessing.

Pray...

Lord, I've often wanted to tell others about You but missed the opportunity. Please give me another chance today, and help me not to miss it.

January 13

I've Been There

 John 11:32–44

I know how you feel when things are difficult. I've been there. I know what it is to be let down by friends or to fight off temptation. I know what it is like when people say things that are not true about you. I know what it is like when a close friend dies. I've experienced all these things and more. And because I went there before you, you can go there now and overcome them all—like I did.

Think. . .
If you are hurting inside, Jesus wants you to tell Him about it so that He can make it better.

January 14

So Much to Say

 Luke 18:31–34

I've got so much I want to share with you, so many things I want to tell you. Some things will take a while to understand, but that's OK— let's keep walking and talking.

Pray...
Please help me to understand Your teaching and Your stories in the Bible.

January 15

Whose Strength?

 1 Samuel 17:33–37

Whose strength shall we use today? Yours or Mine? Who is stronger—you or Me? Shall we use My strength today? Better still, why not use My strength every day!

Pray...
Lord, help me to rely on Your strength rather than my own.

January 16

Little Things Are Important

 Mark 10:13–16

Life can't always be filled with exciting adventures. It's great when special things happen, but simple, little things can be special, too. I enjoy the little things just as much, don't you?

Think. . .
The little things are just as important to Jesus' plan.

January 17

Do My Word

James 1:22–25

Sit in My presence, read My Word, then do what it says. Then you and all your friends will be blessed! What could be more simple?

Pray. . .
Lord, I want to put Your Word into action today.

January 18

Faith

 Ephesians 2:8–9

Faith is the envelope in which you should mail all your prayers to Me. And faith is the strength you need in order to do My will. And, best of all, faith is a free gift from Me to you. You can have as much as you want—just ask!

Think...
Need more faith?
What should you do?

January 19

How Did You Know?

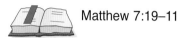 Matthew 7:19–11

Ever received a surprise present from someone and wondered how they knew it was just what you wanted? It's because they love you, they know your needs, and want to make you happy. I know your needs, and I long to make you happy. I have lots of super gifts stored up for you.

Think. . .
What can you give Jesus to show how much you love Him?

January 20

Think Good Thoughts

 Philippians 4:8–9

Think good thoughts, and all day you will be
surrounded by good things. Think bad thoughts,
and all day you will be surrounded by bad
things. Think good thoughts.
Think of Me!

Think. . .
*Why not try and
memorize
Philippians 4:8–9?*

January 21

A Busy Day

 Luke 10:38–42

Who will control your day today: your parents, your teachers, your friends? Don't worry—I'm in control, and I'll keep you safe from harm.

Pray...
Lord, please bring quiet to my busy mind while I pray.

January 22

Don't Give Up

 Philippians 3:12–14

A special mission demands special training. Training can be hard, but it's all worthwhile in the end. I promise!

Pray...
If you are willing to go all the way for Jesus, tell Him.

January 23

Best Friends

 2 Timothy 4:16–18

Can you think of a better Friend than Me? Can you think of a more powerful or generous Friend than Me? I am loving and powerful, and I love to share My strength, My power, My joy, and My riches with you.

Think. . .
Be still and think of Jesus' love for you.

January 24

Need a Hand?

 Luke 5:4–10

Peter, Andrew, James, and John were all good fishermen, but that night they were unable to catch a single fish—until I came along! Need a hand with something?

Think. . .
Is there something you were planning to do on your own that you might need a hand with?

January 25

Peace and Happiness

 Philippians 4:6–7

The way to find peace and happiness is to let Me handle every problem. That way you will be free to enjoy Me and all My blessings. So remember—I'll handle the problems; you handle the blessings!

Think. . .
If you are a worrier, try thanking Jesus for something— daily.

January 26

Many Blessings

 John 6:1–14

How many people do you think you can
bless today with a kind word, a
thoughtful action, or a helping hand? A
little blessing can go a long,
long way! Try it.

Pray. . .
*Lord, please bless
the little that I have
to give.*

January 27

Height of the Storm

 Luke 8:22–25

My greatest power is seen at the moment of greatest need. The disciples thought I was asleep and had forgotten them.
How wrong they were!

Think. . .
Jesus isn't deaf or asleep. He knows your needs already, and He knows exactly what should be done.

January 28

Helping Others

 John 13:1–5

Why did I wash My disciples' smelly feet?
Because I came to serve and to set an example
for anyone who wants to be My friend and
follow Me. Helping others is important. Are you
willing to help those around you? Thank you!

Think. . .
How can I serve best today?

January 29

A House of Rock

 Matthew 7:24–27

Some days can feel a bit rough and wobbly, but you have nothing to fear. No one who puts their trust in Me will ever be let down. Who are you going to trust today? Who are you going to trust tomorrow?

Pray...
Lord, I trust You. Thank You for being there for me and giving me a firm place to stand.

January 30

Inside Out

 Psalm 139:23–24

Things aren't always what they appear to be. And neither are you. I know that sometimes you are smiling on the outside, but inside you are angry and upset. That's not good. Share the problem with Me and let me help–then you can smile on the inside, too. That's good!

Think...
You can be real with Jesus because He knows what you are really like.

January 31

Ups and Downs

 Romans 8:28

Ever tried riding your scooter up a hill? Hard work, isn't it? But then there is the fun of riding down the other side—wheeeeee, what fun! There have to be ups if you want to enjoy the downs; otherwise, life would be very flat!

Pray...
Lord, please give me Your strength to work hard at the tough times so I can enjoy the fun times.

February 1

A Fresh Start

 1 John 1:9

Everybody makes mistakes; that's why My forgiveness is for everyone! So don't fret about yesterday's mistakes. Put them behind you and start afresh today—with My forgiveness and My blessing!

Pray. . .
Lord, I'm sorry for the mistakes I made yesterday. Please forgive me and help me not to make the same mistakes today.

February 2

Practice Love

 1 John 4:7

Loving those who love you is easy. Loving those who don't show you love is harder—and like all difficult things, you need to practice. The more you love, the closer we are.

Pray...
Lord, please help me to love people that are difficult to love— just like You did.

February 3
Your Faith and My Power

 Joshua 6:1–27

What made the walls of Jericho fall down? The strength of men or the might of God? If something or someone is standing in your way, don't worry. Your faith and My power can overcome any problem.

Pray. . .
Lord, please help me to trust You in difficult times.

February 4

Let Go!

 James 2:17

Remember the fun and excitement the first day you rode your bike without training wheels? It was a bit scary at first, but with a little help, you soon got the hang of it. That's real faith. In order to have faith, you have to let go–and let Me catch you if you fall. Wow, what fun, what freedom!

Think. . .
Am I willing to put my trust in Jesus completely?

February 5

Stay Close

 John 15:5

Walk with Me and I will teach you. Listen to Me and I will speak. Don't give in to things that will draw you away from My presence, and you will always know My will.

Think. . .
What could be more important than spending time with Jesus?

February 6

My Longing

 Zephaniah 3:17

I love it when you are happy to just sit in My presence and be with Me, not because you want something but because you love Me. I love it when you love Me for who I am and not for what I do. Any chance of a hug?

Pray...
Lord, I really, really love You.

February 7
Light in the Dark

 John 8:12

Living in a world of sin is a bit like living in the dark. You need a light to show you which way to go. I'm the Light of the world, and I can show you the way! And, even better, My presence in your heart makes you a light, as well—so you can show your friends the right way to go, too!

Think...
In what ways can you let your light shine for Jesus today?

February 8

Wait

 Isaiah 30:18

Waiting is hard. It would be easier to do something; I know. But if you want to do great things for Me, you *must* learn to be patient and wait for Me to tell you what to do next.

Pray. . .
Lord, if You say wait, I'll wait, because I trust You to answer all my prayers.

February 9

My Voice

 1 Samuel 3:8–10

If you want to hear My voice, you need to listen with your heart, not your ears! Listen. . . .

Pray. . .
Lord, please help me to recognize Your voice in my heart.

February 10

Lifeline

 Psalm 86:7

When troubles, worries, illness, or fears threaten to overwhelm you like huge waves, call to Me for help—I'll be your lifeline from life's storms. Take a firm hold of My hand, and I'll pull you to safety. Trust Me!

Pray...
Lord, it's good to know You are there —always.

February 11

Peace, Be Still

 Mark 6:47–51

Does everything look hopeless? Have you tried everything and run out of energy and ideas? Don't worry; I won't leave you. When things look bad, look up. Don't struggle with problems on your own. Let Me sit beside you.

Pray...
Lord, HELP!

February 12

Meet Me Everywhere

 Jeremiah 23:23–24

Don't just think of Me for a few minutes in the morning and a few minutes before you go to sleep. I'm not just with you in your special place; I am with you everywhere, *all* the time. Let's meet and talk all through the day!

Pray...
Wow! It's great to know there is no-where I can go today that You cannot find me.

February 13

Near the Prize

 1 Corinthians 9:24–27

In a race, it is not the start that hurts or even the long middle part of the course. It is when the prize is in sight that the heart and nerves and courage and muscles are tested the most. Don't be tempted to give in just before you win the prize. Keep going through the tough times— you're a winner!

Pray...
Lord, I'm going to run hard for You. I'm going to work hard and give You my very best.

February 14

In My Presence

 1 Peter 5:7

Things never seem as bad when you spend time in My presence. So, no matter how busy you are, don't forget to spend time with Me.

Think. . .
A problem shared is a problem halved. And if you share it with Jesus, it's a problem solved!

February 15

Super"natural" Man

 Ephesians 6:10–18

The world does not need super-men but supernatural men and women—people willing to clothe themselves in *My* power and not their own.

Pray. . .
Lord, I want to fight wrong and stand up for what is right—just like You.

February 16

Peace and Quiet

 Luke 10:38–42

Hurry, hurry, hurry! Worry, worry, worry! Rush, rush, rush!–whoa! Stop! Hush, hush, hush! Patience, peace, be still. Be calm; wait for Me. A few moments quiet in My presence will reward you with peace to face the day.

Think. . .
Am I too busy to talk to Jesus sometimes?

February 17

Happiness Is. . .

 1 Timothy 6:6–10

What will make you happy: new bike, roller skates, larger TV, more computer games? They may make you happy for a while, but all these things get lost or broken at some point. My love will always make you happy, and it will *never* wear out or run out!

Pray. . .
Never mind what I want. What do You want, Lord?

February 18

Let Me Do It

 Psalm 40:1–2

In a mess? Need a hand? Let Me help!

Think...
Has Jesus saved you from
a sticky situation recently?
Say thank You.

February 19

Patience

 Isaiah 30:18

Don't stop one prayer short of the answer. Don't be tempted to run ahead without Me. I won't fail you. I will answer your prayer—in *My* time. Patience.

Pray...
Oh, Lord, please give me patience to wait for Your answers to my prayers.

February 20

No Need to Beg

 Philippians 4:6

If you want what I want, then I want what you want. So all that you ask for I will give you, because we want the same thing! If it is good for Me, then it is good for you! So there's no need to beg; just ask!

Think...
What does Jesus want? Is my goal the same as His goal?

February 21

This Way. . .

 Psalm 119:105

In the dark? Can't see where you are going? Not sure which way to turn? Let Me help. Let Me show you the way, one step at a time.

Think. . .
Jesus is the Light of the world, so I never need fear the darkness because He is always with me.

February 22

Doubts Delay

 Hebrews 3:8–19

The children of Israel would have arrived at the Promised Land a lot sooner—only their doubts and fears held them back in the desert. Doubts delay; trust is the way!

Pray...
I'm sorry if I doubt You sometimes, Lord.

February 23

The "Buzzy" Life

 Psalm 128:1–2

The busy life is a joy-filled life!
Let's work together today.

Pray...
What shall we do today, Lord?

February 24

Share Everything

 2 Corinthians 9:6–8

Share your love, your joy, your happiness. If you want more of these, give them away and I'll give you all you need. The more you give, the more you'll get. Try it!

Pray...
Lord, please give me an opportunity to give some love or joy away today.

February 25

How to Conquer

 2 Thessalonians 3:3

Jesus saves! Jesus reigns! Jesus is Lord!
Shout it out loud to every doubt or fear or
temptation that comes your way, and
watch them run!
Jesus reigns! Hooray!

Think...
*Jesus saves! Jesus reigns!
Jesus is Lord! Hooray!*

February 26

Rags to Riches

 Matthew 6:25–34

A king doesn't worry about clothes to wear or food to eat. And neither should you, because you are a son or daughter of the King—and all that I have is yours to share.
So don't worry—ask!

Think...
What does it mean to be a son or daughter of the King of Kings?

February 27

Seek My Touch

 Matthew 8:14–15

Remember how I touched and healed in the Bible? I am no different today. All that I did then I can do now—and more.
Simply ask.

Think. . .
Do you know someone who needs Jesus to touch them and make them better?

February 28

Grow, Grow, Grow

 1 Peter 2:2–3

Food is great! You need lots of food to grow up healthy and strong. A good breakfast will supply you with all the energy you need for the day. Time spent with Me can supply you with energy, too. The love, joy, peace, and guidance that you find in My presence will give you spiritual strength to face the day ahead. Breakfast?

Pray...
I want a double helping today, Lord! Please!

February 29

Draw Near

 Matthew 23:37

I love you *sooo* much. That's why I came to earth –so that we could be friends. If only you knew how much your friendship really means to Me– if only the world knew!

Think. . .
Jesus longs to be with us more than we long to be with Him. Wow!

March 1

Listen!

 1 Samuel 3:1–19

So many people call out to Me, and I hear every word, but so few people wait for My reply! I have so much to give. I can help in so many ways, but only those who listen will ever know. Remember—prayer is a two-way conversation. Let's talk. . .

Pray. . .
Speak, Lord, I'm listening.

March 2

Even Greater Things

 John 14:12

There's no way you could imagine the things I have planned for you. My disciples did amazing things for Me, and I'll help you do the same, because you are My special friend, too.

Pray. . .
Lord, I want to do great things for You.

March 3

Grow Like Me

 John 8:12

The more time we spend together, the more alike we become. The more we talk and you read My Word, the more you see what I see, feel what I feel, and do what I do. You may not notice how alike we are, but your friends will. Let's spend more time together!

Pray. . .
Lord, I like spending time with You. Thank You for always being there.

March 4

Seeing Things My Way

 John 15:15

People don't always see thing the way I see them. Like the time Peter tried to stop Me from going to the cross. All he could see was the pain and suffering, but I could see past that to new life and hope for all! You know Me and My ways; try and be patient with people who don't see things as clearly as you do. . . .

Pray. . .
Lord, please help me to see things the way You do.

March 5

Do Not Fear

 John 14:27

Don't look at the things that make you afraid;
look at Me—I'll make you strong and fill you with
love and joy and peace and confidence!

If you are afraid or worried, talk
to Me. I'll listen and I'll
answer. (Don't forget to wait
for My reply!)

Think...
*Jesus says "do not be
afraid" 366 times in the
Bible. That's one for
every day of the year!*

March 6

Love and Laugh

 Zechariah 4:6

Don't work against Me by doing things in your own strength. Work with Me by doing things in the strength that My Holy Spirit gives. That way you won't get worn out, and you will manage to do so much more! My strength makes work easy, not difficult.

Pray. . .
Lord, please help me to do things in Your strength today.

March 7

Surprises

 John 2:1–10

I love planning fun surprises for My friends, like the time I cooked breakfast for the disciples by the lake or the time I supplied wine for the wedding feast. I love to see people happy. I love it when you laugh.

Pray...
Help me to make You smile today.

March 8

Heaven Now!

 Matthew 19:14

The joy of heaven starts here! All the good things of heaven came into your heart when you said *"yes"* to My friendship. Eternal life, peace, love, joy. . .it's all yours to enjoy *now*–today!

Pray. . .
Thank You for dying so that I could enjoy eternal life–today.

March 9

Nothing Is Too Small

 Matthew 10:42

Nothing is too small for Me to see. Nothing escapes My attention. One kind word is more precious to Me than a whole speech by an important person. Don't be fooled into thinking that big is best!

Pray. . .
Please help me to get the little things right today.

March 10

Laughter Travels

 Mark 4:30–32

SPLASH! Have you ever thrown a pebble into a pond and watched the ripples spread out in all directions? Your kind thoughts and actions are a little like that pebble. The joy they bring spreads out in ever-increasing circles around you. Want to create a few ripples today?

Think...
What can I do to make someone happy today?

March 11

A Reflection of Me

 Matthew 5:16

My prayer is that when people look at you they
will be able to see Me, just like they saw
My Father when they looked at Me
and saw My actions.

Pray. . .
Lord, make me the
answer to Your
prayer.

March 12

Keep It Simple

 Matthew 22:37–40

Love Me; love My ways. Don't be tempted to make it any more difficult than that.

Pray...
Lord, please help me to love what You love and to do what You do.

March 13

Power to Live

 Luke 3:21–22

If you want to do all that I did, you need to be filled with My power—the Holy Spirit. The Holy Spirit helped Me to do My special work, and He will help you to do the same—and more!

Pray...
Lord, please fill me with Your Holy Spirit so that I can do Your work.

March 14

Big Hugs

 Psalm 73:28

Sometimes, especially when life is hard, we need a hug from someone who we know loves and cares for us. Somehow it gives us strength and helps us to face the day.
Want a hug?

Pray...
Thank You for loving me and for always being there when I need You.

March 15

Lighten Up

 Luke 15:11–32

Wrong thoughts and actions can feel like a heavy weight around your neck. Don't waste time and energy carrying them around with you all day. Simply say *"I'm sorry,"* and you will be free to enjoy life once again.

Think...
Is there something that you need to make right or say "I'm sorry" for? Ask Jesus to help you, and He will.

March 16

A Quiet Place

 Mark 6:45–46

Do you have a special place that you go to when you want to be quiet and alone? I often needed to find a quiet place away from people where I could think and pray. Next time you go to your place, can I come, too? Can we make it our place? Can we meet there soon?

Pray. . .
If You needed to be alone to pray, then I certainly do. Please help me to find time to talk to You.

March 17

What's Mine Is Yours

 Luke 11:10

Don't look at the little you have and worry. Look at all that I have, know that it is yours, and be happy! I give freely to all those I love when they need it.
I love you!

> **Think. . .**
> *God made the earth and all that is in it. It all belongs to Him!*

March 18

Think Big

 Isaiah 40:28–29

I'm *big*. I can do *big* things. Nothing is too *big* for Me to handle. I love giving *big* blessings. What's the biggest blessing I could give you?

Pray. . .
Lord, please help me to think BIG!

March 19

Trust Me

 Numbers 23:19

I'm here. I will never fail you. I never break a promise. I have power enough and love enough for all your needs. Trust Me—I won't let you down—promise.

Pray...
Thank You for being with me yesterday, today, and always.

March 20

Little Things. . .

 John 6:1–13

Big trees grow from little acorns. In the same way, the little things that I ask you to do or say can achieve great things. Trust Me and do the little things, and you never know what might happen.

Pray. . .
What would You like me to do today, Lord?

March 21

Are We Nearly There Yet?

 Joshua 1:9

I wonder how many times you have asked that question on a long journey in the car? Sometimes, getting somewhere or something seems to take forever. But don't worry; be patient; I know where we are going and, yes, we have enough fuel to get there. So sit back and enjoy the ride!

Pray...

Lord, please help me to be more patient!

March 22

Ask Me

 Matthew 7:7

Who is the richest person in the world? Who is the strongest? The most powerful? My riches are greater, and My power is stronger by far. There is nothing that I can not do and no need that I can not meet. Ask Me!

Think...
If God made the world, is there anything He can't do?

March 23

Pray, Pray, Pray

 Luke 11:5–10

Don't stop praying; the answer will come. I hear every word. I know that you love Me, and I know that you trust Me, so be patient. Sometimes My answer is *"yes,"* sometimes My answer is *"no,"* and sometimes My answer is *"not yet."* So sometimes you will have to wait and see!

Think...
Is there something you need?

March 24

Why?

 1 Corinthians 1:25

I wonder where you go to get the right answer to your questions—a grown-up, your teacher, a book, the television? Why don't you come to Me? I have all the answers to all the questions you could ever ask.

Think. . .
The Bible is God's instruction Book for life.

March 25

Little by Little

 1 Peter 2:2

How tall are you? How tall were you yesterday? How tall will you be tomorrow? It's hard to believe, but one day you'll be as big as the grown-ups around you. Growth happens slowly. You can't see it, but day by day you're growing. And day by day you're getting more like Me. Imagine that!

Pray. . .
I want to grow up to be just like You.

March 26

Follow Your Guide

 Jeremiah 29:11

Don't worry about tomorrow, or you won't enjoy today. Trust Me as your guide. I know what lies ahead. Hold My hand and let's take the next step together.

Pray...
With You by my side, I have nothing to fear—thank You.

March 27

Keep Going

 Matthew 8:23–27

Relax! Nothing is bigger
and no one is stronger
than Me! And I am
always with you.

Pray...
*Lord, please
give me Your
strength for
today.*

March 28

Mountain Moving

 1 Samuel 17:45

Big problem? No problem! Trust in My Word, do what it says, and all things are possible— even moving mountains! But you must do both —trust and obedience go hand in hand.

Think...
Is there something you need to do that seems as impossible as moving a mountain? Ask Jesus to help you and then get to work!

March 29

Be a Champion

 Matthew 14:22–31

Training to be a champ takes strength, courage, and a good coach! Trust your coach; I'm rooting for you and am always there to encourage you through the tough times–when you grow the most. Do you want to be a champion? Are you willing to give it a try?

Pray. . .
Lord, please help me to keep my eyes fixed on You today.

March 30

Be Happy; Be Blessed

 Psalm 100:4

Having a bad day? Don't be grumpy; be happy.
Don't say you can't; say we can! Be thankful for
all you have, and let Me bless you. Laughter,
joy, and thankfulness open
the door of blessing.

Think...
*What can I say
"thank you" for
today?*

March 31

I See

 Psalm 139:1–4

I love the little things you do to make other people happy, like those drawings you made and gave away. Others may not always see or understand the love and care that go into them, but I do. Thank you.

Pray. . .
Thank You for understanding me and loving me.

April 1

Transformation

 Acts 4:13

Wow—what a difference! From timid followers to bold leaders. From disappointed fishermen to successful fishers *of* men. They had lots to learn and so do you, but be encouraged; you've got the same great Teacher! Just keep walking and talking. . .

Think. . .
How might people be able to tell that you have been with Jesus today?

April 2

Follow Me

 James 1:22–25

I am with you in just the same way I was with My disciples–to help, encourage, and bless. Follow Me in the same way, and you will grow up to be a miracle-working coworker just like them. Just keep doing the word!

Think. . .
What kind of things would you like to do for Jesus in the future?

April 3

Your Servant

 John 13:5–9

Remember how I washed My disciples' feet to show them I was their servant as well as their Lord? I want to wash your feet today—I am here to serve you, too.

Pray...
Lord, I love Your love! I want to be more like You when I grow up.

April 4

From Faithless to Faithful

 John 21:15–19

Peter wasn't changed in a flash from a simple fisherman to a great leader and teacher. He had to face up to and deal with his weaknesses and learn from his failures. Saying he was sorry and learning from his mistakes, along with a little encouragement from Me, was enough to turn his weaknesses to great strength and courage. Feeling weak? Don't worry!

Pray...
Lord, please change me in the same way You changed Peter–so that I can be a strong and courageous follower of You.

April 5

Your Closest Friend

 Psalm 139:13–16

Feel as though no one understands you? Unable to express how you feel? Don't worry; I understand. I don't look at the outside; I look at the inside. I know how you are feeling and what you are thinking, and I care.
Need a hug?

Pray...
Sometimes I'm tempted to think no one loves or understands me, and then I remember that You do. Thanks.

April 6

Let Go So I Can Give

 Luke 10:38–42

Come to Me with open, empty hands, and I will
fill them with answered prayers. But I can't fill
hands that are already holding onto the cares
and worries of the world!

Think. . .
*Is there some care
or something you
value more highly
than Jesus that you
need to let go of?*

April 7

Change of Heart

John 20:11–18

Before Mary saw Me on that first Easter morning, she was sad, worried, and full of guilt. But all that changed when she met Me in the garden and I called her name! In a moment her heart was renewed and filled with joy, peace, and overwhelming love.

Think. . .
How has your heart changed since Jesus called your name and you met Him face-to-face?

April 8

Be Different

 Matthew 5:13–16

I have called you to be different. Different in the way you live. Different in the way you love. Different in the way you give without wanting back. Different in the way you care and share. Different in the way you speak the truth. Will you dare to be different?

Think...
Have you made a start at all these ways of being different?

April 9

New for Old

 2 Corinthians 5:17

I have changed your heart for a new one—no more thoughts and actions driven by fear and guilt, but thoughts and actions driven by love, peace, joy, and forgiveness. No need to fear the past with all its mistakes; look forward to a future filled with promise—My promise! Yippee!

Pray. . .
Please help me to know that the past really is forgiven and that my future is safely in Your hands.

April 10

Obedience

 John 14:15

Obedience is the key to following Me. Obedience not because you *have* to, but because you *want* to, because you love Me. Obedience and love— do both, and you won't go wrong.

Think...
Has Jesus asked you to do something that you haven't done yet? What should you do?

April 11

Different–Remember?

 Mark 10:45

Remember, I want you to live differently, so that people will see the difference and want to follow Me, too. Different actions, different words, and lots and lots of love!

Pray...
Thank You for making me different.

April 12

Faith Is the Key

 Luke 17:6

Your needs are My opportunity to help. I love helping you. I stand ready to rush to your side. Just a little faith on your part will unlock all the help you need.

Think. . .
Faith is the envelope in which you should mail all your prayers to Jesus. Remember?

April 13

Rejoice!

 Psalm 118:24

Laughter and love can turn the greyest day to pure sunshine! So when faced with a dull, bad, or boring day–rejoice and laugh!

> ### Think...
> If a problem will be worth laughing at tomorrow, why not laugh at it today?

April 14

Look Up

 Proverbs 4:25

How many times have you tried walking along the top of a wall and fallen off? The problem is balance. Fix your eyes on an object ahead and not on the wall, and you will find it much easier. Likewise, when faced with a problem, don't look at the problem. Look at Me, and I will guide you through. Promise!

Pray...
Lord, I'm going to keep my eyes fixed firmly on You today.

April 15

"It's Impossible!"

 Psalm 37:39

Everything out of control. . .head in a spin, butterflies in your stomach. . .life just too much to handle? DON'T PANIC! Stay calm. Take a few deep breaths, and let's talk about it. There is no problem too large or too small for us to handle together. So, what's the problem?

Pray. . .
Please help me not to panic when things go wrong—but to focus on You, like yesterday.

April 16

God Is Love

 1 Corinthians 13:4–7

Make God the center of all you do and say.
God is love. . .no judging. God is love. . .no
anger. God is love. . .all patience. God is love. . .
all power. God is love. . .all you need. . .

Pray. . .
*Lord, all Your ways
are love, so I can
trust You to rule
over my heart.*

April 17

"Lord!"

 Isaiah 65:24

When you call, I come running. I can't help it;
I love you!

Think. . .
*Jesus is waiting for
you to call Him. . . .*

April 18

Love All

 Luke 10:25–37

I want to fill your heart with so much love that you will be able to give some away to everyone you meet. Will you do that for Me? Leave everyone you meet today with a smile on his or her face.

Think...
Jesus wants us to love everyone—even our enemies.

April 19

Who Needs Whom?

 John 15:16–17

You need Me–and I need you. And there are lots of people who need you, too. Why? Because they need to know what you know–and, more importantly, *whom* you know–Me!
Will you tell them?

Pray. . .
Yes, Lord! I'll tell them.

April 20

My Joy

 John 15:9–11

Do you know what pleases Me most and brings Me the greatest happiness? Your patient, gentle, and loving obedience. When I feel your trust in Me, I can't help smiling. Will you make Me smile today?

Think. . .
Obedience is the key to the Christian life.

April 21

Solid as a Rock

 Psalm 62:1–2

Worried about going to a new play group or school? Or maybe something else is changing in your life, like moving to a new home. Don't fear, and try not to worry. All sorts of changes may go on around you, but I will never change. I remain the same yesterday, today, tomorrow, and forever.

Think...
Jesus is your faithful, unchanging Friend, always there beside you. Isn't that great to know?

April 22

Happy Rules

 Deuteronomy 28:13

Imagine playing a game with no rules! It would soon lead to arguing and fighting. You need rules in order to have fun. I give you rules because I want you to be happy and safe. If you obey My rules, life will be good.

Think. . .
God's rules are good rules because God is good!

April 23

Empty Talk

Matthew 21:28–31

Which is more important, what you say or what you do? Which of the two sons pleased his father the most? Why? Actions speak louder than words!

Think...
Have you ever made a promise you haven't kept–to a friend? To Jesus? What can you do to make it right?

April 24

Live Forever!

 John 14:3

It's true! When I rose to life on that first Easter morning, I opened the way to heaven so that we could be together forever. Imagine that! That's something *really* special to look forward to —*especially* when life is hard.

Think. . .
Heaven is the place we will meet Jesus face-to-face. Wow!

April 25

Bless Your Enemies

 Matthew 5:43–48

But I don't want to! He hurt me; she called me names; he doesn't like me; she's wrong. . .
I know what you are thinking and how you feel, and I know you want to set them straight and correct their wrong thoughts and actions, but that's *My* job. Your job is to forgive and bless. You do your part, then I can do Mine. Forgive and bless!

Think. . .
Is there anyone you need to forgive?

April 26

Tired?

 Isaiah 40:29–31

Work, work, work! Play, play, play! Rest, rest, rest! Rest is an important part of the day. Sit and rest a while in My presence, then you will have enough energy for all that work and play!

Pray...
Lord, I love resting in Your presence. I must do it more!

April 27

Seeing Jesus?

 John 20:24–31

Ever wished you had been alive 2,000 years ago so that you could have met Me in person? It would have been fun! But then I could only meet with a few people. Now I can meet with all those who seek My presence daily–including you! And one day we *will* meet together, face-to-face, at My place–in heaven!

Pray. . .
Thank You for the special gift of Your Holy Spirit, who shows me what You are like.

April 28

Follow the Leader

 Luke 15:1–7

Through thorny bushes, across wasteland, through forests, up steep mountains, and down into dark valleys–what adventure! Whose adventure? Your adventure? No, *My* adventure! I'm on a mission to find missing sheep. . .will you join Me?

Pray. . .
Lord, You lead and I'll follow.

April 29

Just Perfect

 Ephesians 3:16–19

Perfect order, perfect harmony, perfect supply of all you need, perfect love, perfect honesty, perfect obedience, all power, all victory, all success! All yours because they are Mine to give. Want them?

Pray...
Yes, please, Lord! I want everything You have to give me.

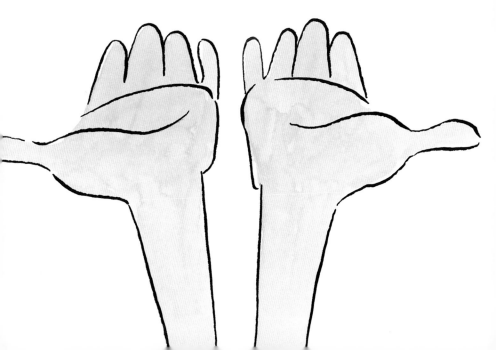

April 30

Signs of Spring

 John 15:5

Spring is a lovely time of year. Buds and blossoms appear on the trees, a sure promise of what is to come—delicious fruit! I can see buds of promise in your life, too. I can't wait to see the fruit! Can you?

Think. . .
What are the buds of promise in your life? And what do you think the fruit might be?

May 1

Answers to Prayer

 Psalm 37:4–7

"Not yet" doesn't mean *"no"*! Delay isn't *"no,"* either. It is simply the time I take to work out your problem and fulfil your desires in the most wonderful way for you. So keep praying. . .

Pray. . .
Lord, I trust You to look after everything and to answer all my prayers in the best possible way –according to Your *will!*

May 2

Arrow Prayers

 Psalm 17:6

Prayers don't have to be long and formal. Prayers can be one sentence or even one word long! If you need My help, fire off an arrow prayer and I'll come running! Just one word— *"HELP!"* will do!

Pray. . .
Thanks, Lord!

May 3

Learn to Forgive

 Mark 11:25

Do you find it hard to forgive? Learning to forgive is a tough lesson, but it must be learned, because if you can't forgive others then neither can I forgive you. That's how important it is.

Think. . . Is there someone I need to forgive or say I'm sorry to?

May 4

Show Me. . .

 Psalm 139:2–3

I love to see what you have been up to. What did you discover today? What treasure did you find? What work have you done today that you are proud of? Or perhaps you fell and cut your knee or someone made you cry.
Show Me. I love to see and share.

Think. . .
What was the best part of today? What was the worst? Thank Jesus and tell Him about it.

May 5

Think!

 Isaiah 51:7

Not all thinking is done in the head. Sometimes it's done in the heart. It's the heart that tells you when you've done something wrong even though your head told you it would be OK. It's your heart that tells you what to do when you love someone but just don't know how to let them know. If in doubt, listen to your heart.

Pray...
Lord, please help me to listen to Your voice in my heart.

May 6

Troubles Shared

 Ecclesiastes 4:9–10

What do you do if you meet a friend carrying a heavy object? Lend a hand, I hope. Troubles can be just as heavy to carry but more difficult for friends to see. If you see a friend in trouble, would you be kind enough to help them for Me?

Pray...
Of course, Lord! Show me someone who needs our help today.

May 7

Miracles Shared

 John 21:5–6

Miracles happen with a little help from you.
The disciples didn't find the fishes already on
the shore; they had to put in a little effort
themselves! I need your effort and you
need My blessing—the perfect
partnership!

Pray. . .
Lord, please help me
to step out in faith
today so that You
can work a miracle.

May 8

Strength

 Philippians 4:13

Difficult task ahead? I promise to supply you with all that you need to complete the task successfully. Trust Me.

Pray. . .
Lord, I'm going to give today my best shot–trusting that You will help me.

May 9

Humility Is. . .

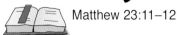 Matthew 23:11–12

Don't be tempted to show off by bragging. . .
"I've got a better bike than you," or "Look,
look, I can do a handstand—I bet you can't!"
Remember that everything you have is a gift
from Me—to bless you and help others.

Think. . .
How can I use
the special
gifts that
Jesus has
given me to
help others?

May 10

Calm Is. . .

 Isaiah 26:3

When disaster strikes, stay calm. Calm is trust in action! First, be still and know that I am God, then act as I tell you. Only perfect trust will keep you calm. Trust Me!

Think. . .
If you find it difficult talking to Jesus, start by thanking Him for something good. . . .

May 11

Never Alone

 Psalm 4:8

We've been through some great adventures together. We've shared some quiet times and some noisy times! Best of friends sharing the best of times, but, unlike friends who have to say good-bye at the end of the day, we never have to!

Think...
Jesus never sleeps! So you can talk to Him anytime!

May 12

Guard Your Treasure

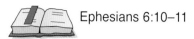 Ephesians 6:10–11

Warning! Doubt, fear, and despair are like thieves waiting to steal your greatest treasures—peace, rest, and joy. So when doubt, fear, and despair come knocking at your door, stand firm and don't let them in!

Pray...
Lord, please guard my heart today and keep me safe.

May 13

Never Judge

 Matthew 7:1–2

Only I can read another's heart. Please don't be too quick to judge another's thoughts, words, or actions. The best thing to do with your concerns is bring them to Me. That way you won't trip into sin.

Think. . .
Are you guilty of thinking wrongly about someone? If so, what should you do about it?

May 14

I Love Hugs

 Mark 10:16

I love it when you ask for help. And I love it when you share your problems, because I love to help you. But most of all, I love it when you ask Me for a hug!

Pray. . .
Lord, I really, really, really, really, really, really love You!

May 15

What's the Plan?

 Proverbs 3:5–6

Where are we going today?
What shall we do? What's the
plan? I have a plan—a perfect
plan, one you're guaranteed to
like! Follow Me!

Pray. . .
Yippee! Let's go, Lord!

May 16

Pray, Pray, Pray. . .

 1 Thessalonians 5:17

Don't stop praying. One day you will see how
your prayers have been answered so completely,
and you'll wish that you had prayed more! So
pray, pray, pray. . .

Think. . .
*The more you
pray the more Jesus
will act.*

May 17

Sorrow to Joy

 Psalm 30:5

Did something bad happen? Be brave. I know that it hurts now, and the feelings are real, but in the morning you will feel a lot better and be ready to smile again. My sunshine always follows the rain.

Pray...
Thank You for being here when I need You most.

May 18

Look!

 Psalm 121:1–8

Imagine what a shipwrecked sailor must feel like when he sees a ship on the horizon! What joy! What relief! What hope! Saved at last! All that because of what he saw. When you are in trouble, need help, or feeling alone, look at Me. One look will fill you with all the comfort and hope that you need!

Think. . .
*Who has the safest
hands in the universe?
Jesus, of course.*

May 19

Safety and Security

 Psalm 40:2

What a great verse; what a great promise—
safety, security, and guidance. Safety: "He pulled
me out of a dangerous pit." Security: "He set
me safely on a rock." Guidance: ". . .and made
me secure"—so that you are free to follow Me!

Pray...
I'm so glad You are
holding on to me
today.

May 20

Winners

 Isaiah 41:10

I'm a winner—so you're a winner! My victory is your victory! So be bold, be strong, and know that I am with you.

Pray...
Lord, I feel so strong and courageous with You by my side. Thank You for choosing me to be on Your winning side.

May 21

Just for You

 Acts 13:1–3

I have many friends, and each one of them is different. I have exciting adventures planned for all of their lives. Each adventure is as different as they are–just as My plans are for you.

Think...

You are totally unique. There is only one of you in the world, and only you can do the special work that Jesus has planned for you. Isn't that exciting?

May 22

What's Mine Is Yours

 Romans 8:16–17

As a child of God, you have the honor of sharing in all that your Heavenly Father owns. No need to beg—just ask. Isn't that fantastic? So, go on—ask!

Think. . .
Is there something you need? What should you do?

May 23

No Buildup

 1 Peter 5:7

Try not to let little worries build up. Use arrow
prayers to set each one before Me as it arises.
That way you will stop small cares from
becoming big worries!

Think. . .
Do you have any little
worries you would like
Jesus to deal with? If not,
spend a little time saying
thank You!

May 24

Give with a Big Heart

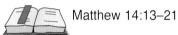 Matthew 14:13–21

The disciples could have chosen to feed only themselves. But by giving the little they had away, they and more than 5,000 others ate their fill. Now, isn't that more fun? You give and I'll bless, or I'll bless and you give!
It works either way!

Pray...
What can I give the Lord today?

May 25

Mission Impossible?

 Luke 1:37

Job too hard? Would I ever ask you to do something that I knew you couldn't do? Never! So if a task seems too hard, maybe it wasn't *Me* who asked you to do it. It might be best to check.

Pray...
Lord, if I try to do something that is not for You today, please show me.

May 26

Time to Grow

 James 1:2–4

Waiting for an answer to your prayer may seem discouraging, but it can be just the opposite. The delay is a great time to learn and grow. It gives Me the chance to test and grow your patience, your faith, your willingness to keep praying, your obedience, and your trust. So you see, while waiting for your answer, you can grow in all these ways as well!

Pray...
Wow! Thanks, Lord, I had never seen it like that. Please help me to make the most of every opportunity to grow.

May 27

Roots and Shoots

 Ephesians 3:17–18

The taller a tree grows, the deeper the roots need to be. Why? Because otherwise it won't be able to stand against the storms. Each time we meet and you read My Word and do what it says, your roots go deeper into Me. So, when the storms come, you will stand up tall and strong.

Pray...
Lord, I want to grow up big and strong. Please help me to understand Your Word and to put it into practice–daily.

May 28

Do You Love Me?

 John 21:15–17

How do I know you love Me? By what you say?
By what you do? How do *you* know you love
Me? By how you feel? What do you feel when
you think of Me? Peace and joy, I hope.

Think...
*Tell the Lord how
much you love Him.*

May 29

Forget Regret

 Psalm 103:12

Feeling regret for past mistakes that have been forgiven and made right is like carrying unnecessary items on a long walk. They weigh, and slow, you down. When I forgive, I forget— so you can, too.

Think. . .
Do you need to let go of a past mistake that is weighing you down? What should you do?

May 30

The Look of Love

Psalm 73:23–24

Talk to Me during the day. Look up into My face
and enjoy a look of love, a feeling of security,
and a feeling of joy as you sense My closeness
to you. These are your best prayers—
and My favorite.

Pray...
*Lord, I love
being with You.
You make me
feel warm inside.*

May 31

Prayer Is. . .

 Matthew 6:7–13

There is more than one way to pray. A word, a thought, an action, a shout, a whisper, a look, a feeling, a sound. . .I hear, see, and answer them all!

Think. . .
How many different ways of praying can you think of?

June 1

Hero Worship

 2 Corinthians 3:18

Do you have a hero? A movie star? A musician? Would you like to be him or her? I'm afraid that's not possible. But if you make Me your hero, I can help you to grow up just like Me! The more we talk and spend time together, the more alike we become. Wow!

Pray...
Lord, I want to be just like You when I grow up.

June 2

Who's Who?

 1 John 3:2

The closer we get, the more like Me you will become, and the more of Me people will see in you. Isn't that great?

Pray...
Please make me more like You, Lord.

June 3

Thank You

 Luke 17:11–19

I love to give gifts. I love it when you say thank You for those gifts. The more you say thank You, the more I like to give you good things. So you keep thanking, and I'll keep giving! Deal?

Think...
Is there something you could thank Jesus for now?

June 4

Here, There, and Everywhere

 Isaiah 40:28–31

I am everywhere! I'm there while you sleep, while
you play, and when you sit quietly. I am always
beside you so I can share your troubles and
failures, and you can share My peace and strength.

Think...
*Jesus is
always only a
prayer away.*

June 5

Sleep Well

 Matthew 18:10

Sleep well; you have nothing to fear. My angels guard you day and night, and nothing can harm you. I promise.

Pray...
Thank You, Jesus, for the times You have been faithful and kept me safe from danger.

June 6

More Than You Need

 Philippians 4:19

Strength, courage, peace, assurance, forgiveness, friendship, joy? Whatever you need—just say the word, and it's yours. I am more than able to supply *all* your needs.

Think. . .
Don't forget to say thank You!

June 7

On Your Marks. . .

 Hebrews 12:1–2

Following Me is like running a race. Picture yourself standing on the winners' podium with a large gold medal around your neck. To run the race and win, you have to keep your eyes fixed on the prize–Me! Are you ready to start running?

Pray. . .
Lord, I want to run for You. Please help me.

June 8

Get Set. . .

 Hebrews 12:3

There may be many ups and downs ahead, but with Me as your coach, how can you fail to win?! I've already run the race, and I'm with you *all* the way—what a team!

Pray. . .
Lord Jesus, thank You that You are my coach, that You are always with me, and that I can talk to You at any time and in any place.

June 9

Go!

 1 Corinthians 9:24–25

Running the race for Me might seem hard at times. You may feel as though you are on your own or that you don't have the courage or strength you need, but don't give up at the first hurdle. Each problem you overcome will make you stronger and fitter and will help you to win –hooray!

Pray. . .
Lord Jesus, please help me to keep going on with You whatever happens.

June 10

Treasure in Heaven

 1 Timothy 6:17–19

A promise kept, a kind word, a thoughtful deed, a loving hug–all add to the treasure that I have stored up for you in heaven. And the more you give–the more you will receive from Me!

Think...
What can you do today that will store up treasure in heaven?

June 11

Peace

 John 14:27

Peace is the feeling you get in your heart when I am near you. No matter how much trouble you are in or how difficult the situation, you can always feel at peace because I am always with you. Faith in My presence brings peace.

Pray...
Lord, thank You for the peace You give in every situation.

June 12

House on a Rock

 Matthew 7:24–27

It takes time to build a strong house on a good foundation. Read My Word daily and do what it says, and you will build a strong house that will last forever.

Think. . .
What kind of a house are you building and on what sort of a foundation?

June 13

What to Do?

 Isaiah 41:10

Don't know what to do? Which way to go? What to say? Look at Me, listen to Me, follow Me, and I'll show you the way. All the time you are looking at Me, I can show you what to do and say. So don't look down—look up!

Pray...
Lord, please help me to read and understand Your Word each day.

June 14

Face Today with Me

 Isaiah 41:13

Let's face today together. No looking back, no shying away from problems—let's march into today hand in hand. Together we will conquer!

Pray...
Wow! Thank You, Lord. I'm never afraid when I am with You.

June 15

Around the Corner. . .

 1 Corinthians 2:9

You can't possibly guess what I have waiting for you around the corner! Such great plans and great blessings—more and greater than you could possibly imagine. Trust Me. Just wait and see!

Pray. . .
Lord, I love You. Thank You for loving me sooo much!

June 16

Let's Talk

 Isaiah 65:24

Don't wait until you are in trouble before you call for My help—talk to Me now. That way, I can help you to *avoid* difficult situations. Let's talk!

Think...
Is there something you need to talk to Jesus about today?

June 17

"Jesus!"

 Acts 3:1–10

You can use My name like Peter did—to heal the sick, to overcome fear or temptation, or as a call for help. Use it tenderly; use it prayerfully; use it powerfully; use it more!

Think. . .
Is there any reason why Jesus can't use you in the same way that He used Peter?

June 18

Wait for Me!

 Luke 10:38–42

Rush, rush, rush! Hurry, hurry, hurry! Too busy to stop, too excited to wait. But hold on a minute; what have you forgotten? Me!!! We can achieve much, much more together!

Pray...
Lord, I'm sorry for the times I leave You behind. Thank You for waiting.

June 19

Keep Going

 Philippians 3:12–14

Don't stop running. Keep going for Me. Don't get sidetracked, or you won't finish the race and win the prize.

Pray...
Lord, please help me to listen to You so I won't get sidetracked.

June 20

Safe and Secure

 Psalm 62:6–7

My love for you is like a castle wall. It keeps you safe and warm and free from harm. Safe and secure in My love, you are free to grow and perfectly protected from all evil.

Think...
Could anything be safer than Jesus' care and love? Is anyone stronger than Jesus?

June 21

Storms

 Genesis 9:12–16

Are you scared of storms? Does lightning frighten you? Do you hide under the covers when the thunder crashes outside? It's not just real storms that can be frightening—problems can seem just as scary. I can't promise that there won't be any storms, but I can promise to keep you safe and help you to stay calm.

Think. . .
Has God ever broken a promise?

June 22

No Way Out

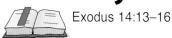 Exodus 14:13–16

Facing an impossible situation?
Can't see a way through? Take
courage and trust Me! Shall
we go together?

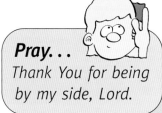

Pray...
*Thank You for being
by my side, Lord.*

June 23

Need Recharging?

 Matthew 11:28

Low on energy? Plug into Me and get recharged!
Rest a while in My presence, and let Me put the
zip back in your life!

Pray...
*I love resting in Your
presence, Lord—it
gives me energy to
face the day.*

June 24

A Gentle Nudge

 Isaiah 48:17

Not sure of what to do? Keep going; I'll let you
know when you should change direction or do
something else. In the meantime, relax and
enjoy the view!

Think...
*What was the last thing
Jesus asked you to do for
Him? Have you done it yet?*

June 25

Your Sunny Friend

 Zephaniah 3:17

Do you have a special friend who always makes you laugh and smile? Who lifts you up when you feel down and fills grey days with glorious sunshine? I do—it's *you*. Do I do the same for you? I hope so.

Pray. . .
Thank You for being my special Friend.

June 26

Slow Down

 Isaiah 30:18

Rush through the day too fast, and you will miss the little things, the quiet things, the important things—like My voice!

Pray...
Lord, I'm quiet now. Please speak.

June 27

Don't Stay Down

 1 John 1:9

Everybody trips up sometime. You get angry, selfish, argue, hurt someone you love. The important thing is not to stay down but say you're sorry, and spring back up on your feet and carry on. Need a hand getting up?

Think...
When Jesus forgives He also forgets. So there is no record of your wrongdoings. Yippee! (If He forgets, then so must you.)

June 28

Celebration

 Psalm 23:5

Hard work deserves a reward! How about a whiz-bang feast—a mega-fantastic supermeal fit for a king? Well, it's all ready for you—dig in; you deserve it!

Think. . .
Expect lots from Jesus and He will never disappoint you.

June 29

Tomorrow Is Mine

 Matthew 6:25–34

Don't spoil today by worrying about the future.
After all, do you know what will happen
tomorrow? No! But I do! So let Me look after
tomorrow *and* you! Deal?

Think...
*Nothing can separate
you from Jesus' love
and care.*

June 30

Pass It On

 Luke 6:38

Blessed, blessed, blessed—bless, bless, bless.
Blessed, blessed, blessed—bless, bless, bless!
I bless you, you bless others, they pass it on,
and everyone gets blessed! So pass it on.

Think...
*It is impossible to
outgive Jesus.*

July 1

Say "No" Like Me

 Matthew 4:1–11

What do you do when tempted to do something that you know you shouldn't? How do you resist temptation? I have the perfect way—with My special sword, the Word of God. Just like Me, you can say *"no"* to temptation by using God's written word in the Bible. It works every time!

Think. . .
Knowing how to use the Bible makes us strong against the enemy.

July 2

Safe Passage

 Psalm 27:1

Difficult day ahead? Not sure how you will get through? Faith is the name of the boat you must use to cross those stormy waters. Faith will carry you safely through to the other side. There is no need to fear at any stage because I am with you. So cast off, and let's go!

Pray...
Lord, with You as the Captain I can laugh at the storm.

July 3

More Than Able

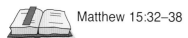 Matthew 15:32–38

If you want to grow up big and strong, you need to eat good, wholesome, healthy food—and lots of it. You never need to worry about having enough to eat with Me as your Friend—just ask!

Pray...
Lord, thank You that I never need to worry that You may not have enough to supply my every need.

July 4

The Perfect Friend

 Ecclesiastes 4:9–10

Think of the perfect friend. . .what would he or she be like? Full of energy, fun to be with, helpful, faithful, generous—always willing to share, encouraging, always on your side, dependable, easy to talk to, always there. . .that's *Me!* I'm *all* of those things and much, much more! Come on, friend, let's go and explore the day. . . .

Pray. . .
*Lord, what shall
we do today?
You choose.*

July 5

Unsinkable

 Isaiah 43:1–3

HUGE waves, as tall as a house, threaten to force the tiny boat off its course, or even sink it. The passengers feel helpless and afraid, but there is no need because the captain is experienced, and steers a straight path through the wind and rain to the safety of home. Trust your Captain; don't look at the wind and waves. Trust Me! I'll steer you through safely—
I promise!

Pray...
Lord, sometimes the waves look really big—but You are bigger! Thank You.

July 6

More Than Able Forever

 Psalm 50:10

I supplied all your needs last year, last month, last week, and yesterday. So what makes you think I won't look after you today, tomorrow, and forever?

Think. . .
The Lord owns the cattle on a thousand hills. He can easily meet your needs.

July 7

Why Me?

 2 Corinthians 4:17

"Why did this have to happen to me?" you might say today. "What is Jesus doing? I thought He was my friend!" I *am,* and nothing has changed. I see everything, and I can use everything to make something beautiful. Trust Me—wait and see!

Pray. . .
It's not always easy, but I trust You, Lord.

July 8

Going My Way?

 Mark 2:14

Are we both going in the same direction? To follow Me you need to do just that—follow! Let Me lead, and I promise thrilling adventures and a worthwhile prize. Come on—I have a terrific day planned. Going My way?

Pray. . .
Yes, please, Lord!

July 9

Why Doubt?

 Zephaniah 3:17

The deeper our friendship becomes, the less you should doubt Me. Day by day, I prove My love for you. Have I ever let you down or broken a promise? NO! And I won't start today! So be done with doubt and fear—trust and pray today!

Pray...
Lord, I'm sorry if I've doubted Your love in the past. Please forgive me and accept my love and trust today.

July 10

Expect Many Miracles

 Acts 4:13–16

When *you* can't, *I* can. When I do for you what you can't do for yourself—that's a miracle. Follow Me, trust Me, obey Me, and you will see many miracles. Ready?

Think. . .
Is there something you need to do that Jesus can help you with today?

July 11

Guardian Angels

 Matthew 18:10

You are the son or daughter of a king. The King of Kings, no less. As a prince or princess, you have a special bodyguard. My angels have special instructions from Me to watch over you and keep you safe from harm. Wow! How does that feel? It should make you feel pretty special.

Think...
Thank Jesus for your heavenly bodyguard.

July 12

Safe and Secure Forever

 John 10:27–28

If I have kept you safe so far, then you must believe that I will always keep you safe—forever and ever. After all, it would be foolish to save a drowning man only to drop him back into the sea again!

Pray. . .
Lord, thank You for saving me.

July 13

Expect the Best

 Matthew 7:11

How do you face the day—full of hope or full of fear? Expecting the best to happen or expecting the worst? Demonstrate your faith in Me today by expecting the best!

Think...
What would you really like to happen today? Tell Jesus.

July 14

In Safe Hands

 Exodus 14:13–16

I protected the Israelites as they crossed the Red Sea because I loved them and had a great plan for their lives. I love you just as much and will protect you in just the same way. So do not fear—I have a great plan for your life, too!

Pray...
Lord, I feel safe in Your hands.

July 15

Afraid of the Dark?

 John 8:12

The dark can be very scary. When it's really dark, you need a light in order to find your way. It's amazing how much darkness a tiny amount of light can chase away. I am the Light of the world. I'll be your Light in the darkness so you can work, rest, and sleep with nothing to fear.

Think...
Jesus said He will never leave you. So His light is with you always.

July 16

A Strong Tower

 Proverbs 18:10

Live, laugh, and trust in My love! Trust in Me produces laughter, because safe in My love you have nothing to fear. My love is a strong tower—a place of security and warmth. Imagine yourself shielded by a strong tower.

Think...
The strong tower of God's love is available for you to run into anytime you feel you need His protection.

July 17

Peace, Be Still

 Matthew 5:1

It was on the quiet mountain slopes that I taught my disciples, not during the storm. Step aside with Me today, and I will show you some of the many things I taught My disciples that day.

Pray...
Lord, I want You to teach me like You taught Your disciples.

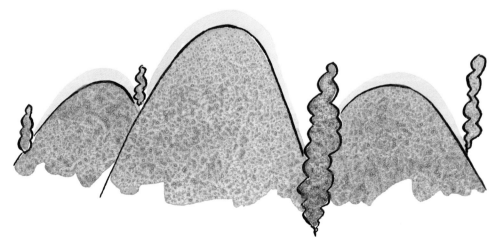

July 18

Walk Humbly with Me

 1 Timothy 4:12

Don't be tempted to change your good ways because of what others might think. Follow Me and My ways, and allow Me to mold your character until you are perfect.

Think...
What Jesus says about you is far more important than the thoughts of others.

July 19

Naturally Supernatural

 Mark 10:27

Miracles are impossible for you but natural for Me. So as a friend and follower of Mine, miracles should become natural for you, too! Expect miracles, but never take them for granted!

Pray...
Thank You, Lord, for all the miracles You have performed for me.

July 20

Teamwork

 Mark 1:16–20

Up a bit, left a bit, down a bit—fire! Bulls-eye every time! Obey My instructions and leave the results to Me. I guarantee we'll hit the target every time. We're the perfect team!

Think. . .
Isn't it great to know Jesus has picked you to play on His team?

July 21

Praise, Praise, Praise

 Acts 16:25–26

Problems, problems, problems. When troubles come, think of all you have to be thankful for and praise, praise, praise. Say, "Thank You" all the time, and *all* your problems will shrink, shrink, shrink!

Pray...
Lord, I want to be just like Paul and learn to praise You in difficult situations.

July 22

You Can Do That

 Luke 9:1–2

Wow! The blind see, the lame walk, the sick are healed, the deaf hear, the dumb speak. . .and I can do it all again (and more) through you if you'll let Me.

Pray. . .
Lord, I want to be just like Your friends in the Bible, and do everything they did for You.

July 23

Peace

 Philippians 4:7

Let nothing trouble your heart. Set peace like a soldier to guard and watch over your heart so that worry, doubt, and fear are unable to trouble you. That way, you will always be able to hear My voice and do the right thing.

Think...
Thank Jesus for His gift of peace, and think how you might use it today.

July 24

Going the Jesus Way

 John 14:6

Stay very close to Me. Think, act, and live in My presence. Relax in My love. Thank and praise Me all the time, and wonder after wonder will unfold. Keep close to Me, and you will always know the way because I *am* the Way.

Think. . .
*Jesus is the Way—
so if you follow Him,
you will always be
going the right way!*

July 25

Wonderful Life

 2 Peter 1:3–4

No worries, nothing to fear, eternal life with Jesus, a guardian angel, peace, joy, forgiveness, hope, security, love, power to overcome any temptation. . .what a wonderful life!

July 26

Forgive and Forget

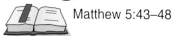 Matthew 5:43–48

Here's a difficult challenge: Let nothing that others do to you change the way you treat them. Treat all as you would treat Me—with love and kindness. Think you can do that? I'll help you.

Pray. . .
Wow! That's difficult, Lord, but with Your help I know I can do it.

July 27

Best Friends

 James 2:23

Sharing, caring, helping, serving, giving, taking,
loving, forgiving, talking, listening, encouraging,
cheering, working, playing, relaxing, supporting,
pleasing, teasing, laughing, crying—
all that we are to each other!

Think...
*Your friendship to
Jesus means as much
to Him as it does to
you—perhaps more!*

July 28

Mistakes

 Philippians 4:13

Never be afraid to make mistakes. They are an important part of learning and a natural part of growing up. Do everything as though you are doing it for Me, and if you don't get it right the first time, try again—and keep trying. Give it your best shot, and no one can ask for more.

Think. . .
Jesus is on your side. He wants you to grow and is rooting for you all the way.

July 29

Overcomers

 John 16:33

The world is not like heaven. It is not always an easy place to live. Troubles will come, but stay cool. I have overcome the world and all its problems. Live in the power of My love, and you, too, will know the joy and peace of overcoming.

Think...
When things look down, look up and ask Jesus for help to overcome.

July 30

Faith Rewarded

 John 20:24–29

Down through the ages, there have been many who have not seen Me but chose to believe and follow Me, including Noah, Abraham, Joseph, Moses, Joshua, David, Thomas, and you! Everyone receives a special reward for his faith in Me. And that includes you, too!

Think. . .
Wow! Imagine sharing the winners' podium with all those famous people!

July 31

Practice "Thanks"

 Psalm 105:1–5

There is always something to be thankful for,
even after the worst of days—a kind word, a job
well done, a beautiful flower, a blue sky. . .
When life seems hard, seek out the things to be
thankful for, and joy will spring up
in your heart once more.

Think. . .
*Make a list of things
you are thankful to
Jesus for and use it
to thank Him!*

August 1

Stuck Like Glue

 Romans 8:38–39

Imagine sticking two objects together with the strongest glue in the world so that they become inseparable. That's like us. There is nothing in the whole universe that can pull us apart!

Pray...
Lord, that is so reassuring to know that You are stuck on me just as much as I'm stuck on You.

August 2

Prepare the Ground

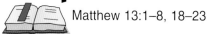 Matthew 13:1–8, 18–23

I love to sow seeds of blessing. *You* prepare the soil and *I'll* put in the seeds. Then *together* we can enjoy the harvest.

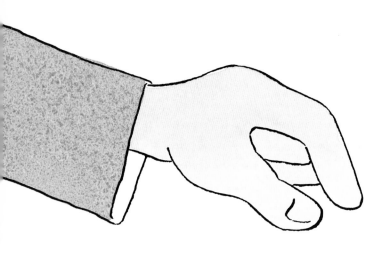

Think...
Prayer fertilizes the soil. The more you pray, the richer the soil of your heart will become.

August 3

The Most Precious Gift

 Psalm 27:4

What do you think the most valuable gift you could give Me might be? The one thing I would like more than anything else? No! It isn't something that can be bought or made! Give up? It's your time! Those special moments you set aside to be with Me.

That's what I value the most.

Think...
Plan times through the day when you can spend just a few moments alone with Jesus.

August 4

Just the Beginning

 John 17:3

Getting to know Me now is just the beginning!
We are going to spend eternity together. Think
of the biggest number you can, then add a
thousand zeros to it, and multiply that number
by itself again and again and again! Dizzy? Even
that number isn't big enough to describe the
length of time we will have together.
Isn't that fantastic?!

Think. . .
*In heaven you will
be able to see Jesus
face-to-face.*

August 5

Hour of Need

 Matthew 6:8

The moment you need help, I'm there. No distance to travel. No time delay. Before the words leave your mouth, I am by your side. No waiting; no worry!

Think. . .
You don't have to plead with Jesus to help you. He knows your need before you do.

August 6

Refill Time

 Matthew 14:23

If I needed quiet moments to draw aside and pray, then I think you do, too. Time to recharge the batteries, time to refill the jug so that you can go on pouring out My love to others in so many different ways.

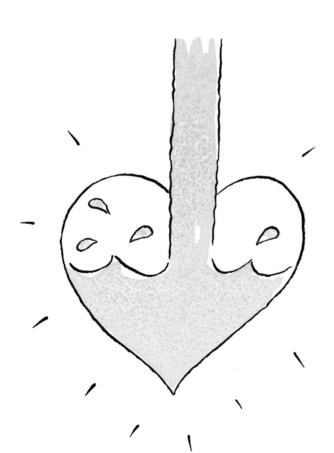

Pray...
Lord, I do feel a bit tired sometimes, as though I have nothing to give. Please fill me up afresh with Your love and joy and strength.

August 7

All Yours

 Numbers 23:19

The strong, protective arms of My love, My words of encouragement and guidance, and My power to save are always immediately available for you—but you must ask!

Think. . .
When in need, don't forget to ask.

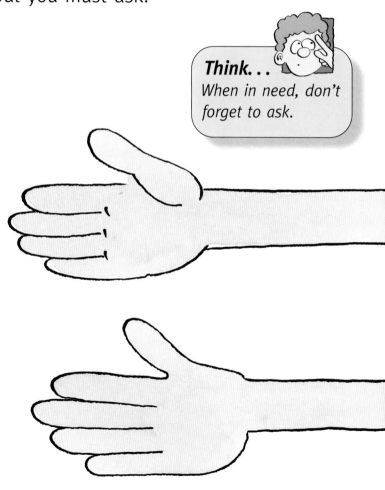

August 8

Pouring Out Blessing

 1 Kings 17:8–16

The more you give away what little you have inside, the more I will fill your heart and life with good things. You pour, and I'll continue to fill. That way, no one runs out of blessing!

Pray. . .
Lord, fill me up until I overflow!

August 9

Jesus—Number One

 Proverbs 3:1–6

Don't be tempted to follow the world's ways—
the latest games and toys or the *"me first"*
crowd! Draw near to Me, and let Me reassure
you that My ways are sure and My paths are
safe and straight. Don't let the world tempt you
onto the wrong path.

Think. . .
Is Jesus number one in your life?

August 10

Stray Sheep

 Luke 15:4–7

That little sheep got lost because it wandered away from where it could hear My voice. As soon as it heard My voice again, it called for help. Stay close to Me, and you won't get lost!

Pray...
Lord, I'm going to stay especially close to You today–so that nothing will come between us!

August 11

Sticky Situation

 Genesis 1:1–2

How are you at sorting out sticky situations? Solving problems creatively is My speciality! If I could order the whole world out of vast chaos, rest assured I can easily untangle your stickiest problem—no sweat!

Pray...
Lord, it really is great to have You as my Friend, always on hand when I need You, and so clever!

August 12

Change the World

 Matthew 6:10

No prayer goes unanswered. If you see a situation that is wrong and needs to change, bring it to Me in prayer. You can talk to Me about anyone and anything. My love can change the hardest heart and most difficult situation. Together we can change the world. You ask, and I'll answer!

Think. . .
Praying gets things changed to go Jesus' way. Look out for situations or people who need your prayers today.

August 13

Be Perfect!

 Philippians 1:6

Every day I am helping you towards the goal,
from dark to light, weakness to strength, danger
to safety, little to plenty, wrong thinking and
doing to right thinking and right doing. . .
Look how far you have already come and be
encouraged–but don't stop there. Let's keep
going!

Think. . .
Not sure what the
right thing to do is?
Ask yourself what
Jesus would do–
and then do it.

August 14

My Richest Gift

 John 10:10

Full, abundant, overflowing, joyous, powerful—LIFE! Free to all who care to ask and receive it. Nothing held back, everything laid before you for your blessing!

Pray. . .
Thank Jesus in your own words for His amazing gift of life.

August 15

No Fishing!

 Micah 7:19

When I forgive the wrong things that you have thought or said or done, I wipe them out as though they never existed. They get thrown into the deepest sea where no one can find them, including you—so no fishing!

Think...
Is there something that you have said or done that was wrong that you need to say you're sorry for? Remember you only need to say you're sorry once!

August 16

Take It Easy

 Matthew 11:28–30

Hey! I never expect you to work alone! My plan is that we do *everything* together. So take a break, rest a while, then let's go tackle the job together. OK?

Think...
Four hands are always better than two—especially when two of those hands belong to Jesus!

August 17

Sunshine and Fresh Air

 Psalm 67:1–7

Don't you just love it when the sun shines?
Everybody seems happy and relaxed. Sunshine
and fresh air make great medicine! So do trust
and faith. Turn on the sunshine and fresh air of
My presence with a little trust and faith, and
banish those grey days for good!

August 18

The Truth Within

 1 Samuel 16:7

How often have you gone to church thinking, *I don't want to go to church today; it's boring,* or sung the words to a hymn but not meant them? It makes Me really sad when your heart doesn't match your actions or your words—because I look at your heart.

Think...
What does Jesus see when He looks in your heart? Is it shiny and clean, or is there something you need to say you're sorry for?

August 19

True Worship

 John 4:21–24

You don't have to go to a special building or use special written words to worship Me. True worship comes from the heart—a heart that longs for My presence and seeks My face. And every heart that worships Me I fill with wonder, love, and strength.

Think. . .
You can worship Jesus anywhere, anytime and in any way. Even here and now! So what are you waiting for?!

August 20

A Fresh Start

 John 21:15–17

After his betrayal, poor Peter had to face his own weaknesses before I could make him strong enough to follow Me and do My work again. His courage was small and his doubt was great. He meant to be strong and brave, but he knew he was weak and timid. But all that changed when I forgave his past and renewed his hope for the future. Do *you* still love Me? Don't let past mistakes separate us.

Think. . .
If you trip up, don't stay on the ground and pout. Get up and finish the race with new strength.

August 21

Loved to Bits

 2 Corinthians 5:17

Look at that old broken teddy, his fur worn away by years of love. What shall we do? Throw him away? Never! He's far too precious. Let's mend him and make him as good as new!

Pray...
Lord, I think I might have a few worn patches that need mending...

August 22

Learn to Laugh

Psalm 42:11

If you will laugh about today's troubles tomorrow, why not laugh at them today? Let the sunshine of My love turn all your tears to laughter—today!

Pray...
Lord, it's hard to
stay unhappy when
I start to think
of You.

August 23

Onward and Upward

 Philippians 3:12

How do you climb a mountain? One step at a time! Every step you take today, no matter how hard or small, brings you closer to the top. Hooray! What a view awaits those who make it to the summit!

Think. . .
Take today one step at a time—with Jesus, of course.

August 24

All Things Are Possible. . .

 Mark 10:27

All things are possible with God. All things are possible with God. All things are possible with God. Found something you think is impossible? *All* things are *possible* with God! Got it?

August 25

Tired Is OK

 Isaiah 40:29–31

Tiredness is not a sign of weakness. Tiredness can follow a job well done, a race well run. Tiredness tells the body to rest a while before starting the next job. Tiredness is OK.

Think. . .
If you are really tired, how about going to bed early and asking Jesus to give you an extraspecial good night's sleep?

August 26

From Bad to Good

 Romans 8:28

It's hard to believe I can use trials and troubles for good, but it's true. I know how you feel; I suffered My share of trials and troubles, and look how I triumphed in the end. Trials and trouble are a part of this world, but if you keep your eyes on Me, I can show you the way through and make sure they are used for good in the end.

Think...
If anyone can bring good out of bad, it's Jesus—trust Him.

August 27

No Pain, No Gain

 Hebrews 12:5–11

Have you ever had a shot? Did it hurt? Maybe just a little? You might think quite a lot! But the discomfort of the needle is nothing compared to the disease it prevents you from catching. It's hard to trust the doctor when you know it might hurt, but he has your best interests at heart, and so do I. Do you still trust Me? Even when things are rough?

Pray...
Lord, I can trust You in the hard times because I know You are working for my best.

August 28

I Love You

 John 15:13

I love you so much there isn't anything I wouldn't do for you. How much do you love Me?

Think...
How many different ways can you show Jesus you love Him today?

August 29

I'm Here

 James 4:8

Unsure of today? Place your hand in Mine and gently squeeze—then I will wrap your hand in Mine and carry you through the day.

Pray...
Here's my hand, Lord.

August 30

Give, Give, Give!

 Mark 10:17–31

I say, "Give! Give! Give!" You say, "Give what? What? What?" I say, "Your time, your comfort, your love, your happiness, your joy, your sympathy, and so much more." I say, "Give! Give! Give!" You say?

Think. . .
Look out for people and situations that you can make better today.

August 31

World Changers

 John 15:1–8

I need your prayers to change the world. I have prayers I want you to pray. Snuggle up close to My heart and hear it beating for the world. Please pray My prayers so that together we can change the world.

Think...
See a need? Don't know what to pray? Think what would Jesus want to happen in this situation? Then pray the answer.

September 1

How Rich You Are

 Hebrews 13:5

My love, understanding, and strength will never leave you. Forever you are assured of love, strength in every difficulty and danger, and in every situation (no matter how hard), you will always have someone who understands to lean on and talk to. How rich you are.

Pray...
Forgive me, Lord, when I complain that I do not have enough, when I have all this.

September 2

I Must Provide

 Psalm 145:13–16

A king commands the obedient service of his people. In return, he is bound to fight for, plan for, protect and provide for their every need. Such is My responsibility for you.

Pray...
Lord, please help me to trust You more for the small as well as the big things.

September 3

Savior

 Matthew 1:21

Savior—that's My name and it's what I do best! I can save you from anything: fear, care, pain, sorrow, doing wrong, and anything that could cause you harm—anything! What can I save you from today?

Think. . .
The name Jesus means Savior.

September 4

Drop Those Burdens

 1 Peter 5:7

When you bring Me your burdens, the troubles and worries that weigh you down, and drop them at My feet, leave them there. Don't pick them up and take them with you when you go!

Think...
Oops! Am I still hanging onto burdens that I have already given to Jesus?

September 5

Keep Growing!

 Philippians 1:6

Yesterday you were strong, brave, and loving. Today—be stronger, braver, and more loving! And tomorrow—more still. Why? Because you can! Because I will help you. Because I want you to grow in these ways every day!

Pray. . .
Lord, I want to be stronger, braver, and more loving than yesterday. Let's go for it!

September 6

Unseen Helpers

 Psalm 91:11–12

We all know angels live in heaven, but where do they work? Yes, in heaven, but here on earth, too! They have special instructions from Me to help all My friends in all sorts of ways. So next time you need help, it might just be an angel who comes to your rescue. So keep your eyes open!

September 7

Father's Arms

 Psalm 32:7

Where do you feel safest? In your house? In your bed? In your father's arms? No place is as secure as a father's arms. Let Me put My arms around you today. Feel secure? You should!

Think...
Jesus is bigger than any problem you face.

September 8

Smile!

 Psalm 36:7

My love and care for you cannot be measured.
There simply isn't a tape measure long enough!
My love and care for you cannot be described;
there simply aren't enough words!
So smile—that says it all!

Think...
Can you think of some
good words to say
thank You for Jesus'
love and care?

September 9

Success

 Hebrews 6:10

What is success in the eyes of the world? Fast cars, latest fashions, a big house, nice vacations, lots of money, top job, big parties. . . What is success in My eyes? Helping a friend, giving to the poor, serving people in need, using your special talents to help people, putting others first, being content with what you have. . .

September 10

Choose

 Luke 16:13

Which kind of success are you going to choose to follow—the world's or Mine? They both offer you a rich reward, but you can't have both. The world's riches will only last a lifetime, but Mine will last forever!

Think. . .
Have you made a decision yet? What was your answer?

September 11

I Am

 John 15:5

I am, so you are, too! I am Love and Joy and Peace and Strength and Power and Healing and Humility and everything else you see in Me. If you are joined to Me like the branches to the vine, then all these things are you, too. Because if *I am*. . .then *you are,* too!

Think. . .
Think of all the things Jesus is. Make a list.

September 12

Money

 Luke 19:1–10

Money isn't bad. But it does have to be handled very carefully. And it must never become more important than Me. If you choose to make lots of money, that's fine. Just make sure that you do lots of good things with it; otherwise it will be bad!

Think. . .
Can money supply all your needs? What about happiness, joy, forgiveness, freedom from guilt, miracles? NO! Only Jesus can supply all those!

September 13

Jesus! Jesus! Jesus!

 Philippians 2:9–11

Say it softly–"Jesus!" Shout it out loud–"Jesus!"
Call My name urgently–"Jesus!" Whisper it in
love–"Jesus!" Cry for help–"Jesus!" Finish a
prayer–"Jesus!" Encourage a friend–"Jesus!" Use
it everywhere–"Jesus!"

Think. . .
Jesus isn't a magic
word to get what
you want. Jesus is
the most wonderful,
powerful, beautiful
name in the whole
universe! Use His
name with care.

September 14

Unbelief?

 Mark 9:23–24

I love to answer this prayer for more faith. More faith, more answers to prayer! More answers to prayer, more miracles! More miracles, more faith! So don't hide your unbelief away. Give it to Me, and ask for more faith in return. I love to answer that prayer!

Pray...
*Lord, I do believe—
help my unbelief.*

September 15

Take a Break

 Isaiah 30:15

Relax. Take a break. Rest a while. Take the chance while you can to let Me renew your strength by taking all your worries and fears. Be quiet. Be still. Be comforted by Me for a while.

Think...
Is there somewhere quiet you can go when you need a break?

September 16

Work at Rest

 John 15:4–8

Not all success is achieved by running around and working hard. You can bear lots of fruit by resting in Me. Sow in prayer, water in trust, and reap with joy. What could be simpler?

Pray...
Lord, I want to learn how to achieve more for You, by listening to You.

September 17

Stepping-stones

 Psalm 32:8

Have you ever had to use stepping-stones to get across a river? It's a bit scary seeing all that water flowing between them. You might feel unsafe, but I can assure you they are very secure. I would never have brought you this way if I thought it was dangerous. Trust Me? Good, let's go!

Think...
Do you trust Jesus not to lead you into danger? Will you follow Him today?

September 18

Hideout

 Psalm 91:1–10

Do you have a hide-out? Somewhere you go when you want to hide away? A tree house, a favorite bush, under the bed? I've got the best place imaginable where you can hide out. . .in My arms! No one can touch you there, and it's always warm and dry and very, very safe!

Think. . .
Lord, I love the thought of being held in Your arms, especially when I'm asleep.

September 19

Treasure Hunt

 John 15:11

Searching for buried treasure is great fun.
Following the clues and searching out the
hidden jewels along the way is exciting. The
teaching I gave to you and My disciples is rich in
jewels. Seek them out, and you will be rich in
joy all your life! Let joy be the buried treasure
you search for in life.

Think...
*Reading God's Word
(the Bible) daily is
the best way to find
His jewels.*

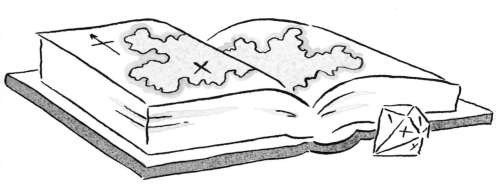

September 20

Taste and See

 Psalm 34:8

"I hate ice cream!" Can you imagine someone saying that? Usually it's because they are not willing to try it. I think that is very sad. God is good, really good, incredibly good, brilliantly good —much better than ice cream! Taste and see!

Think. . .
Do you have a friend who doesn't love Jesus yet? How could you encourage your friend to have a taste?

September 21

My Father and I

 John 14:7–11

You say, "What is God like? Why can't I see Him?" I say, "You can! You have!" If you've seen Me, then you have seen My Father. He is just like Me, loving, merciful, powerful, forgiving, wise. . . everything that I have shown you!

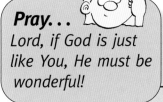

Pray. . .
Lord, if God is just like You, He must be wonderful!

September 22

Sing!

 Psalm 95:1–5

Sing Me a song–a happy song, a song of praise, a song that will thrill My heart and fill Me with joy. And as you sing I'll fill *your* heart with love and joy. Sing!

Think...
Sing!

September 23

Turn to Me

 James 4:8

If you think you have wandered off and left Me behind, don't worry. I'm right behind you, just a whisper away. Simply turn around, and we'll walk back together until we find the right path once more.

Think...
Have you left Jesus behind? Do you need to say you're sorry?

September 24

Do what?

 John 14:6

"Do this," "do that," "say this," "say that," "go here," "go there". . . Everyone is telling you to do something different. What should you do? Follow Me. I am the Way, the Truth, and the Life. Do what I say, and you won't go wrong.

Pray. . .
Thank You for Your instructions in the Bible that help me to know, do, and say what is right.

September 25

Rush, Rush, Rest!

 Matthew 11:28

Rush in, rush down your dinner, then rush out to play again! That's no way to rest—you'll soon run out of energy that way. Rush in by all means, but take time to pause and eat. That way, you'll avoid running out of energy—and getting a tummyache!

Think. . .
Don't be tempted to rush in and out of Jesus' presence. Take time to rest and enjoy His company.

September 26

Serve

 John 13:14

Serve, serve, serve. When you serve, you are doing My work, and that should make you glad. It should fill your heart with joy. It fills My heart with joy! Thank you.

Pray...
Lord, it's fun doing Your work. What would you like me to do today?

September 27

How Much Do You Want?

 2 Kings 4:1–7

If you bring Me a thimble, I will fill it. If you bring Me a bucket, I will fill it. If you bring Me a swimming pool, I will fill it! There is no shortage of supply. How much you receive is up to you! How much do you want?

Think...
What do you need? How much do you want?

September 28

No Returns

 Luke 6:27–36

Sometimes I may ask you to do things for people who will give nothing in return. This might seem hard to you, but when you do this you share in My great work. To give and not expect to receive something back is worthy of My highest praise and greatest reward.

Pray...
Lord, I am happy to serve You today, no matter what it costs.

September 29

The Gentle Touch

 Psalm 23:1–2

Sometimes it is good just to know someone else is there. Just his or her presence is enough; no words need be spoken. A firm touch on the shoulder brings reassurance. A light touch on the arm gently shows the right way to go. And at night, a gentle hand laid on your head quiets your mind and blesses you.

Pray. . .
Lord, it's really, really good to know that You are always there.

September 30

Keep the Change

 Philippians 4:13

Your mother would never send you to the stores without giving you enough money to pay for all the items on her list. That would be foolish!
In the same way, I would never ask you to do something for Me unless I knew I could supply all you needed to carry it out.
And that's a promise!

Pray...
Lord, please give me everything I need today.

October 1

Ask, Ask, Ask

 Luke 11:5–13

When you see someone in need and feel unable to help, ask Me to help. Ask, ask, ask; and I will bless, bless, bless!

Think. . .
Pray for someone you know who needs Jesus' help.

October 2

Lead On

 Proverbs 3:11–12

Ever taken a puppy for a walk? He scampers this way and that, tugging in every direction but the one you want him to go in. So excited by the sights, sounds, and smells around him that he is quite unaware of danger. Your will and your hand keeps the puppy safe. Isn't that a bit like you and Me sometimes?!

Think. . .
When we disobey Jesus, we can end up hurting others as well as ourselves.

October 3

Peace

 John 14:27

Peace comes from knowing that you have done and said the right thing. Peace comes from knowing that nothing stands between us. Peace comes from knowing that your future is safe in My hands.

Think. . .
How does Jesus' peace make a difference in your life?

October 4

True Beauty

 Isaiah 53:2

I wonder what first attracted you to Me? What made you want to be My friend? What did you hear about Me? What did you read? My beauty is on the inside, not the outside. All that I do and think and say comes from My heart of love.

Think. . .
How would you describe your Friend Jesus to someone who had never met Him?

October 5

Divine Appointments

 Psalm 121:8

A chance meeting with a friend. Bumping into an elderly neighbor in need of help. A tiny bird on the path in need of a gentle hand back to its nest. No, not chance! One of My divine appointments!

Think. . .
Keep your eyes and ears open for divine appointments today.

October 6

Simple Trust

 Psalm 18:1–19

You cannot imagine the thrill I get when you place your tiny hand in Mine. How could I ever fail to honor your trust in Me?

Pray...
Lord, I want to follow You today.

October 7
Hidden Strength

 Exodus 4:10–12

Don't let your weaknesses get you down—they should encourage you! Why? Because when you are weak I am strong. Your weaknesses give Me an opportunity to show My strength through you. You may feel weak sometimes, but I am always strong! And I can make you strong, too! Try Me!

Think...
Jesus will always give you the strength to do His will–always!

October 8

Look at Me

 Matthew 14:29–31

Looking at the problem can make it appear big, big, bigger! Looking at Me will always make it small, small, smaller. Look at Me, not the problem!

Pray...
Lord, I know when things get me down, and I'm so wrapped up in my own problems, I fail to see You at work. Help me to open my eyes.

October 9

Love

 1 Corinthians 13:6–7

Take a few moments to think about all that we have been through together. . .the joys, the sorrows, the difficulties and the successes, the hardships and the easy times, the dangers and ultimate safety! That's love!

Pray. . .
Lord, thank You for Your love that keeps me safe. I know that I can always trust You—especially through the hard times.

October 10

Trust

 Proverbs 3:5–6

Put your hand in Mine day by day. Allow Me to guide you and help you. That's trust!

Think...
Don't try to live for Jesus on your own. Trust Him for everything.

October 11

Praise First

 Matthew 6:9

"I've got a problem!" Praise! "But I need Your help!" Praise! "But I'm feeling sad!" Praise! Praise! Praise! "OK, You win; I'll find something to be thankful for. . . Hey, You know what? I feel better!" I knew you would. Now, what's the problem?

Pray. . .
Praise! Praise! Praise!

October 12

Greatest Gift?

 Mark 10:13–16

What's the best gift that you have
ever been given? A bike, roller
blades, trip to the ocean?
Would you like to know My
best present of all time?
It's *YOU!*

Think...
*Why do you think
Jesus loves you so
much? Why do you
love Jesus so much?*

October 13

Steps of Faith

 Acts 3:1–10

Faith is like a mountain. The higher you climb, the more you can see. And the more you can see, the more you can believe. Make each day a step of faith. Ready?

Think...
A small step of faith or a giant leap? Which will it be today?

October 14

No Going Back

 Psalm 103:12

Don't keep returning to the mistakes of the past.
Once handed over to Me, they are forgiven and
forgotten. I've forgotten them, so you should,
too. Now doesn't that feel better?

October 15

Immeasurable Wealth

 Psalm 24:1–2

Can you measure the wealth of a king? Imagine all his greatest riches in one huge pile–all his gold, silver, houses, servants, food, land, clothes, cars, coaches. . .what a sight! So much wealth! But I am the King of Kings, and My wealth goes far beyond that; and it's all available to you–just ask.

Think. . .

Wow! Jesus is bigger and greater and more wonderful than anything we can imagine. He made the earth and everything in it–including you!

October 16

Praise!

 Psalm 23:1–6

Unhappy? Worried? Fretful? Fearful? Sorrowful?
Feeling down and can't see a way through?
Praise! That's right, praise! Turn your eyes to Me,
and fear turns to faith, sorrow turns to joy,
worry turns to peace, and helplessness turns to
patience. So praise!

Pray. . .
Use Psalm 23 as a prayer.

October 17

A Good Example

 Acts 4:13

Don't look at your unrest—look at My calm and My rest. Don't look at your impatience— look at My unfailing patience. Don't look at your imperfection—look at My perfection. Look at Me, and you'll grow like Me, and all your friends will know that you have been with Me.

Pray. . .
Lord, You're my hero! I want to be just like You.

October 18

Loneliness

 John 16:32

I understand loneliness and rejection. I understand what it feels like when friends leave you in your hour of need. I know it hurts when no one will play ball. I know what it feels like inside when people laugh at you. So come to Me when you feel lonely. Your friends may reject you, but I never will.

Think...
How do you feel when friends let you down? How did Jesus feel?

October 19

Hear My Answer

 1 Kings 19:11–12

I answer *every* prayer you pray, but not always in the way you might expect. I might answer in a way you thought wasn't possible. Trust Me, wait for My reply, and don't limit My answer by your own imagination, or you might miss it!

Pray...
Speak, Lord–I'm listening!

October 20

You're Never Too Young

 1 Timothy 4:12

You don't have to wait until you are all grown up to follow Me and do My work. I have a plan for everyone—young and old! I can use you in lots of different ways to help lots of different people. I need you—just as you are! Ready?

October 21

A Special Guest

 Revelation 3:20

Who's coming to dinner today? How will you prepare to meet your special guest? What will you eat? How will you decorate the table? What will you wear? Is everything ready? Are you excited? Knock, knock! Who's that at the door? May I come in?

Think...
How well prepared is your heart to receive Jesus today? Do you need to do some tidying up?

October 22

A Warm Heart

 Philippians 4:8–9

Fill your heart with good things—things that are beautiful, good, and true. Make your heart a comfortable place for Me to live—warm and welcoming. Fill it with love and joy and peace. . . .

Think. . .

Peace comes from knowing Jesus is comfortable in your heart. Perhaps you need to say you're sorry for something?

October 23

Faith

 Matthew 8:5–13

Faith can mean waiting for the last moment
before getting My answer. Faith is being sure of
My love and care when others have given up
all hope. I always reward faith.

Pray. . .
*Lord, I want to
learn to trust
You more—
especially in the
hard times.*

October 24

Being Different

 John 13:34–35

My love in your heart makes you different—
different for all to see. I want you to be different
so that others will see and want to be like you,
and follow Me, too.

Think...
Don't try to be like
others. Be different.
Be like Jesus.

October 25

No Time to Waste!

 Hebrews 12:1–3

There's so much to do, so many places to go, people to meet, things to tell you, so much to see. There's no time to waste or fear of boredom. So leave the TV. Let's do something that will change the world!

Pray...
Lord, please help me to do the things that are important today.

October 26

Love Hurts Sometimes

 John 18:25–27, 21:15–17

Being let down by a friend hurts, *really* hurts–
because you trusted your friend. *All* My friends
let Me down when I needed them most–and it
hurt, but I forgave them, and now we are the
very best of friends again.

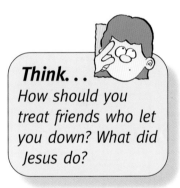

Think. . .
*How should you
treat friends who let
you down? What did
Jesus do?*

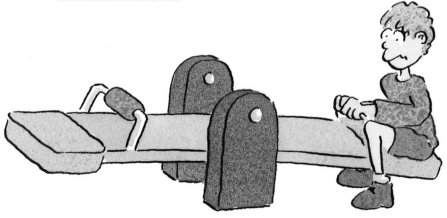

October 27

Do Your Best

 1 Corinthians 10:31

Do your best—that's all I ask. Your best is good enough for Me. Your best might mean coming in second or third in a race or only getting six out of ten for your spelling test. But if you did your best, that's all that counts, and you're a winner in My eyes.

Pray...
Lord, You always give Your best for me. I'm going to do my best for You today.

October 28

A Nice Surprise

 Matthew 7:11

Close your eyes and put out your hands. . .that's how you should pray. So close your eyes and put out your hands—I have a surprise for you!

Pray. . .
Ask the Lord for a surprise today. Don't forget to thank Him!

October 29

Well Done!

 Matthew 25:14–21

What did you do really well today? How do you know you did well? Did someone tell you? Your mom, dad, a teacher, or friend? Or maybe you think nobody noticed? Well, I did! I'm so proud of you when you do well. I'm especially proud when you do My will! Let Me give you a big hug!

Think. . .
What special talent has Jesus given you? How can you use it for Him?

October 30

Patience

 Romans 12:12

Patience is a gift. If you lack patience, ask Me and I will supply all you need—but you might have to wait!

Pray...
Lord, You are very patient with me. Help me to be as patient with others.

October 31

Dear You. . .

 2 Timothy 3:16

Use My special Book of instructions (the Bible) to help you each day. It tells you all about Me, how much I love you, and how to get the very best out of life by doing what is right. Think of it as a letter from Me each day, full of encouragement, good advice, and lots and lots of love!

Think. . .
Everything Jesus wants you to know is in His Word—the Bible! Everything!

November 1

Simple Prayer

 Matthew 6:5–8

When you pray, talk with Me. Don't make it complicated like some grown-ups do–keep it simple. Long words won't impress Me and twist My arm. Simply talk to Me from your heart, and I will answer you from Mine.

Think. . .
Prayer isn't magic or like making wishes. It's simply talking to Jesus!

November 2

Let It Flow

 Luke 6:38

What could be better than a jug of ice-cold lemonade on a hot summer day? *Sharing* a jug of ice-cold lemonade with your friends on a hot summer day! That's *really* great! Share all that I give you, and you will have many friends. Need more lemonade? Give Me your jug, and I'll fill you up again. There's plenty more where that came from.

Think...
The more you give away what Jesus gave you, the more He'll give. What could be better?!

November 3

Make My Day

 Luke 11:9

Imagine My disappointment if you don't ask
for anything—especially since I have promised
to give you everything you need to follow Me.
So go on, make me happy—
ask for something!

Think...
*Is there something
you need? Talk to
Jesus about it.*

November 4

"Jesus"

 Psalms 145:17–19

Call My name often: "Jesus." Not because it will bring Me to you—I am already by your side—but because it will help you to know that I am there and gives Me the opportunity to say "Yes!" So call My name often.

Pray...
Jesus! Thank You for loving me, for being my Friend, and for always being there.

"Yes!"

November 5

Unfinished Business

 Luke 4:43

I can't rest until My work is finished. I want everyone to know about Me and to become My friends so that we can all share eternity together. I can't rest until everyone knows. . . will you help Me?

Pray. . .
Who would You like me to tell today, Lord?

November 6

Something Good?

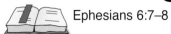 Ephesians 6:7–8

Did anything good come out of today? Did you learn something new? Did we talk? Did you help someone? Did someone help you? Answer "yes" to any of these questions and, *yes*, something good *did* come out of today. Something good comes out of every day spent with Me!

Pray...
Thank Jesus for the good things that happened today.

November 7

Showing You Care

 John 11:33–44

Finding the right words to say or right thing to do to help a friend can be really tricky sometimes. But there are times when you don't need words. Just being there is enough. And, remember, wherever you go—I go, so you can always offer your friend My help, too.

Pray. . .
Lord, You always said and did the right things. Please help me to follow Your example.

November 8

Forgiven!

 Isaiah 43:25

Don't keep a record of past failures and wrongs, yours or anyone else's. Erase them with love, just like I did—at the cross.

Think. . .
Tomorrow is a new day in which you can start again to do what's right and to do better.

November 9

Making Friends

 Luke 19:1–9

Think about your best friend. How did you become friends? Why did you become friends? How did you become *My* friend? Why did you become My friend? I love you, too! For all the same reasons— and more!

Think. . .
Jesus longs to be with you even more than you long to be with Him. Isn't that great?

November 10

Something New

 Jude 24

How did you learn to ride your bike? I suspect there were a few falls along the way, but nothing too serious because you had someone to help you. Would you say it was worth taking the risk? I hope so! Never be afraid to try something new for Me—I'll help you.

Pray. . .
Lord, if You are able to keep the whole world safe, I know You are more than able to help me.

November 11

The Big Picture

 2 Corinthians 4:17–18

Some things are really hard to understand, like friends leaving, pets dying, getting the flu, a broken arm. But all these things are like dark tiles in a huge mosaic picture that can only be seen from a distance. Trust Me. One day you'll stand up here with Me, and I'll show you the whole picture of your life. You will be so amazed at what you see!

Pray...
Ask Jesus for faith to trust Him even when you can't understand why things happen.

November 12

No Words, Just Me

 Isaiah 46:4

Sometimes you don't need words of comfort.
You just need to know that someone is there—
someone who loves you and can comfort you
deep inside. No need to say a word;
I'm always there.

Think. . .
*Sit with Jesus a
while and let Him
comfort you.*

November 13

Come to Me

 Matthew 17:24–27

Never be afraid to approach Me. Come to Me for the answers to all your questions—I never tire of the question "why?" Come to Me to calm your fears—especially at night. Come to Me for all your needs. Come to Me for everything—

I am always here.

Think...
Talk to Jesus about your greatest need—or the greatest need of a friend.

November 14

Follow the Instructions

 Exodus 20:1–17

You can get into a fine mess by not following the instructions, like baking a cake with salt instead of sugar–YUCK! To avoid making a mess of life–follow the Maker's instructions!

Think...
Jesus has written everything down for you in His special Manual–the Bible! Read it daily and you won't go wrong!

November 15

The Same Jesus

 John 20:30–31

Have you read about Me in the Bible? Have you read about the adventures I had with My disciples and friends? I haven't changed. I am just the same and can do all those things today —if you trust and believe in Me. So, what shall we do today?

Pray...
Wow! I want to go on adventures with You—just like the disciples did.

November 16

One, Two, Then Three

 Matthew 18:20

Two are better than one, and three are better than two. For especially difficult problems, try praying with a friend. I've never been known to miss a prayer meeting.

Think...
Praying with a friend encourages your faith. Do you have a friend you could pray with?

November 17

Small Things

 Matthew 25:23

A cheery smile, replacing a trash can lid, taking the blame for something you didn't do. . .small things that could easily go unseen, but I see and reward every good deed that you do. Wow!

Think. . .
If Jesus can trust you with the little things, He can trust you with the big things!

November 18

Let It Shine

 Matthew 4:14–16

When you are kind, gentle, loving, truthful, joyful, patient, and forgiving, your life shines—just like Mine.

Pray... *I'm going to shine like a beacon for You today, Lord!*

November 19

The Source of All Blessing

 Psalm 121:1–2

As you dip your toes in the clear, cool, refreshing stream of My love, look up to the mountain above from where it flows—to the source that supplies all your needs.

Think. . .
Don't worship the gift; worship the Giver of the gift! Don't worship creation; worship the Creator!

November 20

Questions

 Isaiah 65:24

Why? How? When? Where? What if? Wow—so many questions! It'll take a lifetime—and more—to answer them all, but I will! It's a good thing we've got eternity together; I think we'll need it! Now, what was that first question again?

Think. . .
Do you think there is a question Jesus cannot answer?

November 21

Smile!

 Matthew 5:14–16

Don't hide the joy that springs from following Me. Smile out loud so that all the world will know about our friendship!

November 22

Love Is More

 1 Corinthians 13:1

A simple word spoken in love means more than a thousand words spoken without love. Unsure what to say? Say something simple—with love.

Think. . .
If your heart is full of love, you will always have something to say.

November 23

It's Not Fair!

 John 16:33

Life isn't fair. Bad and sad things do happen sometimes. Life won't be perfect until you reach heaven. In the meantime, you must learn to take My hand and let Me walk you through the bad times. There is nothing we cannot face and overcome together.

Think. . .
God never intended sin to be a part of the world. It all began when Adam and Eve decided to go their own way.

November 24

Learn to Serve

 John 13:12–17

I served people in big ways and in small ways. Sometimes everyone saw, and sometimes no one saw. Big or small, seen or unseen, all your acts of service are important because you do them for Me, and I reward them just the same.

Pray. . .
Who can I serve on Your behalf today, Lord?

November 25

Knock, Knock

 Revelation 3:20

I don't force My friendship on anyone. I wait patiently, longing to help and encourage, but only when invited. I long to be friends with everyone, if only they would be friends with Me.

Think...
Have you got a friend who doesn't know Jesus yet? How about introducing them?

November 26

The Real Me

 Psalm 86:5

Some people think I am unloving, angry, make bad things happen, and don't care about the world. . .but that is because they don't really know Me. If they knew the real Me, they would discover that I am not like that at all. Can you help them to discover the truth about Me?

Think. . .
How can you show people what Jesus is really like?

November 27

Love Is the Key

 John 14:23

Don't trust and obey Me because you *ought* to. Trust and obey Me because you *want* to— because you know I love you, would give My all for you, am big and caring, and wise and loving. Trust Me because I love you and you love Me.

Think. . .
If you feel you can't trust Jesus for something, pray for a greater understanding of His love so that you can.

November 28

Unhelpful Things

 John 15:1–4

Once a year, the gardener cuts out the old dead wood and branches that bear little fruit, so that new, healthy fruit-bearing branches can grow in their place. Then there will be lots of fruit for everyone to enjoy.

Pray...
Lord, if there are any unhelpful things in my life that are stopping me from bearing fruit for You, please take them away.

November 29

Yes!

 Matthew 18:19

What a great promise! When two of My friends agree together about something they know I would approve of–I am bound to answer their prayer–fantastic! But I need to hear your request, so don't forget to pray it!

Think. . .
Jesus is waiting for you to pray so that He can answer.

November 30

Feeling Guilty

 Isaiah 1:18

You can hide from your friends. You can hide from your parents. You can hide from your brother or sister. But where can you hide from yourself when you feel like a failure, when you feel weak and want to cry, when you feel guilty? You can hide in Me. Cuddle up close and tell Me all about it— then I'm sure you will feel a lot better.

Think. . .
Jesus' door is always open, and you can talk to Him about anything.

December 1

Marks Out of Ten?

 Mark 6:35–44

My disciples got ten out of ten for seeing the people's need, but zero out of ten for *meeting* it! If you see someone in need, offer help—not just words or thoughts of sympathy. And if you can't help or don't have the answer, I usually do —as My disciples discovered!

Pray...
Lord, please give me the faith in You to meet people's needs in the same way.

December 2

I Am. . .

 Colossians 1:15–22

King of Kings. Mighty God. All powerful. All knowing. All seeing. Ruler of heaven and earth. Creator of all things. . .your friend.

Pray. . .
Lord, I love You for who You are and not just for what You do.

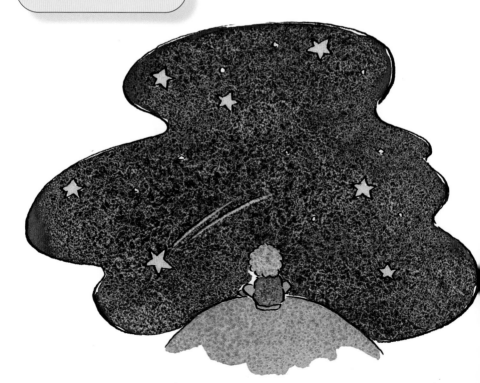

December 3

Stay Cool

 John 15:18–26

Sadly, not everyone wants to be My friend and, sadly, sometimes they can cause trouble for those who are. They might call you names or reject you because you follow Me. When someone is mean to you because of Me, don't fight back or call them names. Simply turn away and pray for that person so that she might become a friend of Mine, too. Now, wouldn't that be cool?

Think...
How should you act toward a friend who turns her back on you? How did Jesus react?

December 4

Oh, Dear

 Isaiah 53:5

Oh, dear. It wasn't your fault, but you're the one they shouted at. And they didn't even give you a chance to explain. I know what it feels like to take the blame for something you didn't do–it hurts. I took the blame and turned it into something wonderful. Would you like Me to do the same for you?

Pray...
Lord, thank You for understanding when others don't. Please take away my angry feelings and replace them with love.

December 5

What to Give?

 Galatians 5:22–23

What have you got to give? Well, let's see. . .
what have I given you that you could give away
to others? Love, joy, peace, patience, kindness,
goodness, faithfulness, gentleness, forgiveness,
friendship. . .and much, much more! So what
have you got to give away today?

Think. . .
*Is it possible to out-
give Jesus? Try!*

December 6

Expect Temptation

 1 Corinthians 10:13

The temptation to do or say wrong things will always come your way. It's impossible to hide from it, but it's not impossible to say "NO!" Temptation only becomes sin when you give in— so say "NO!" to temptation and "YES!" to My help! I will always show you a way out if you ask Me to.

Think. . .

Jesus doesn't want you to do wrong, but if you do He is always ready to forgive you if you turn to Him. YES!

December 7
Spiritual Growth

 John 4:31–34

To grow up physically strong, you need to eat physical food. To grow spiritually strong, you need to eat spiritual food. Praying and reading My Word is a good start, but the real meat is doing My will. That's what you need to give you spiritual strength and muscle.

Pray. . .
Thank You, Lord, for food—both kinds—food for my body and food for my spirit.

December 8

My Kingdom

 Matthew 6:10

My kingdom is anywhere that I rule. It is certainly in heaven. It can also be here on earth where people put Me first, and in your heart when you follow My will. My kingdom is growing every day as more and more people become My friends and choose to follow Me.

Think. . .
A kingdom is where a king rules and his people obey him. Is Jesus' kingdom in your heart? Home? School?

December 9

Me First?

Luke 18:18–30

Whoops! I don't think he got the answer he was expecting, but he got the answer he needed to hear! I knew he couldn't follow Me until he put Me first. I knew that deep down inside money and possessions were more important to him than My friendship. How about you?

Think. . .

Do you love Jesus more than anything else in the world? Why do you think it is so important to put Jesus first?

December 10

Practice What I Preach

 James 1:22–25

You have heard many things from Me. But hearing and doing are very different. I want you to put into practice what you have heard. So rather than Me talking, take a few moments to think about what you have learned recently, and then think about how you can put some of those things into practice—today!

Pray. . .
Please give me the opportunity today to show You what I have learned.

December 11

The Gift of Today

 Psalm 118:24

Have you ever got up early to watch the sunrise
—the sky filled with color, light spilling out in all
directions as I unwrap a new day? A gift for you
to enjoy—a whole new day to play in. What
shall we do?

Pray...
*Thank You, Jesus, for
the gift of today.
Please help me to
use it wisely.*

December 12

No Fear

 1 John 4:18

It is impossible for light and dark to live together. Turn on the light, and the darkness disappears! Love and fear cannot live together, either. Perfect, trusting love overcomes all fears. So when fear comes, turn on love—turn to Me. Love Me and fear will disappear!

Pray...
Thank You, Jesus, that the light of Your presence is always with me—even in the darkest places.

December 13

Relax and Enjoy!

 1 Corinthians 2:9

Do you like surprises? Like a mystery day out? What fun, what joy, what excitement! You know the day will be filled with great things because it has been planned by someone who loves you. I have a great future planned for you—how exciting! What fun!!

Think...
Is there anyone you can trust more than Jesus?

December 14

Storms

 Acts 27:13–44

Storms can be scary things. Next time there's a storm, close your eyes and imagine that you are in a cool garden with sweet flowers and bees and butterflies and trees and fountains in the middle of a busy city. A place of peace and beauty in the midst of all that noise. When everyone around you is losing their cool and shouting, don't join in —be that garden for them.

Think. . .
Jesus can't promise that there won't be storms in our lives, but He does promise to stay with us through them.

December 15

Hidden in the Shadows

 Psalm 36:5–9

Playing in the sun is great. But too much sun can be harmful. So every once in a while you need to sit in the shade and cool down. When I sense danger, I cover you with My shadow so no harm will come to you.
I'm your good shadow!

Pray...
Lord, You are soooo wonderful! Thank You!

December 16

Joy Is. . .

 Psalm 16:11

Joy is knowing I am always there. Joy is knowing you are always loved. Joy is knowing that I'm smiling with you. Joy is knowing that I am crying with you. Joy is My special gift to you that no one can take away—ever!

Think. . .
Are you feeling joyful today? If not, why not? Isn't Jesus' love enough to fill you with joy?!

December 17

Simply for You

 Matthew 18:1–4

My kingdom is made for children. In fact, grown-ups have to become like little children to know Me and My kingdom. Grown-ups make things *sooo* complicated when it's *sooo* simple! Simple trust, simple faith, simple obedience, simple truth! All the blessings of My eternal kingdom—simply for you!

Pray...
Thank You for making me so special and giving me a special place in Your heart.

December 18

Now, Today!

 James 2:5

Let's explore the riches of My kingdom: no violence, anger or hatred, tears or pain, but love, joy, peace, comfort, healing, freedom, forgiveness, friendship, laughter, and so much more. And you don't have to wait until you reach heaven. You can have it all now, today —if I reign in your heart.

Think...
Have you asked Jesus to reign in your heart? If not, why not do it now?

December 19

Guard Your Heart

 Titus 2:11–14

Saying "No!" to temptation can be really difficult —especially when it is something that you really want to do. But if you say "Yes," "No" will be even harder the second time! So say "No!" the first time, then turn and race into My arms, and together we will go and find something far more exciting to do!

Pray...
Use the prayer Jesus taught His friends in Matthew 6:9–13.

December 20

Is There No Hope?

 Psalm 142:1–7

Tired and grumpy and fed up! Nothing looks good; everything looks bad. Nobody loves you; everybody hates you. . .uh, excuse Me, can I come in? *I* love you (even when you're grumpy!), and *I* care about you and your day. And I'm ready to listen—when you are ready to talk.

Pray. . .
Lord, I know I shouldn't really feel this way. Please forgive me and help me to change.

December 21

Large and Small

 Matthew 14:13–14

I created the dainty snowdrop and the mighty oak tree. I enjoy the small, gentle things as well as big, strong things. I enjoy the quiet times and the noisy times. What about you? What shall we enjoy today? We could enjoy them all if you like!

Think. . .
Walking with Jesus doesn't mean less—it means more! There's so much to enjoy!

December 22

I'm the Biggest

 Isaiah 40:21–24

Large and small fears are the same to Me. I can
blow them away with a gentle puff of My love.
As big as your fear might seem, it's not as big
as Me—not by a long way. Look at Me
and laugh at your fear.
Come on, let's have a
hug-friend!

Think...
*Jesus is more than a
billion times bigger
than your biggest
problem! Yippee!!*

December 23

Peacemaker

 Matthew 5:9

Two of your friends are arguing. . .
"It's mine!" "No, it's not, it's mine!" "Well, I had
it first!" "No, you didn't!" Oh, dear, what can we
do? How can we help? I hate to see friends
fighting, especially over such a silly thing.
Christmas is a time for peace and love. I wonder
what would make them really happy?
I know—let's share some of
that ice-cool lemonade.

Pray. . .
*Fill me up today,
Lord, so I have
lots to give.*

December 24

Small Beginnings

 Luke 2:1–7

No trumpets, no grand palace, no servants, not even a warm room or a comfortable bed. Pause and wonder. . .

Think. . .
Is there room for Jesus in your heart this Christmas?

December 25

Happy Birthday

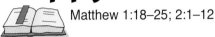 Matthew 1:18–25; 2:1–12

The wise men brought Me gold, frankincense, and myrrh. What could you bring Me? Bring Me the same. . .

Gold–your wealth
Frankincense–your worship
Myrrh–your willing heart

Three gifts fit for a king!

Think. . .
In all the rush and fun of Christmas day, don't forget to thank Jesus for His gift, and give Him yours.

December 26

The Gift Goes On

 1 John 3:16–18

I came to serve—to offer help, hope, and comfort. Not to look after My own needs, but the needs of others. It's the gift I brought to the world—the one I give to you and hope that you will give to others. . .the gift of love.

Think. . .
Who could you serve a portion of love to today?

December 27

Stay on Track

 Deuteronomy 31:8

Following Me really is the greatest adventure you will ever have. Don't let others tempt you away from Me onto a different path. Encourage them to come along with us!

Think...
Life with Jesus is just too good to keep to yourself! Invite a few friends to come along on the adventure.

December 28

Fact or Feeling

 Ephesians 3:17–21

I am with you. You may not always feel My presence, but My company does not come and go with your feelings. My promise given is kept. I am with you–always. Your forever Friend–fact!

Pray. . .
Thank You for caring and always being there–even when I think You're not!

December 29

Prayer Works

 Mark 2:1–5

Prayer leads to action. You pray, and I'll act! But you can help, too. You don't have to leave all the work to Me. What could you do to help answer your prayer for your friend?

Pray...
Lead me to someone who needs our help today, Lord.

December 30

Something for Everyone

 Romans 10:8–15

Oh, dear! Look at all these unopened presents.
If only people knew what was inside—My love,
joy, peace, forgiveness, strength, protection,
help. If you told them, they might want to come
and receive their own free gift from Me. Will you
do that for Me?

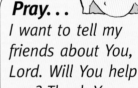

Pray...
*I want to tell my
friends about You,
Lord. Will You help
me? Thank You.*

December 31

Jesus Is Everything!

 Psalm 138:1–8

Jesus—forgiver of *all* your sins, large and small. Forgiver of doubt and impatience, anger and worry.

Jesus—Savior and Friend, joy bringer and rescuer, Leader and Guide.

Jesus—deliverer from fear, from attack, from failure, from weakness.

"Jesus!"—say My name often—"Jesus!"

Pray...
Think back through the year and thank Jesus for His faithfulness and care.

Contents

 If a subject or day was particularly special for you, mark the box as a reminder.

April

- [ ] Transformation
- [ ] Follow Me
- [ ] Your Servant
- [ ] From Faithless to Faithful
- [ ] Your Closest Friend
- [ ] Let Go So I Can Give
- [ ] Change of Heart
- [ ] Be Different
- [ ] New for Old
- [ ] Obedience
- [ ] Different–Remember?
- [ ] Faith Is the Key
- [ ] Rejoice!
- [ ] Look Up
- [ ] "It's Impossible!"
- [ ] God Is Love
- [ ] "Lord!"
- [ ] Love All
- [ ] Who Needs Whom?
- [ ] My Joy
- [ ] Solid as a Rock
- [ ] Happy Rules
- [ ] Empty Tank
- [ ] Live Forever!
- [ ] Bless Your Enemies
- [ ] Tired?
- [ ] Seeing Jesus?
- [ ] Follow the Leader
- [ ] Just Perfect
- [ ] Signs of Spring

May

- [ ] Answers to Prayer
- [ ] Arrow Prayers
- [ ] Learn to Forgive
- [ ] Show Me. . .
- [ ] Think!
- [ ] Troubles Shared
- [ ] Miracles Shared
- [ ] Strength
- [ ] Humility Is. . .
- [ ] Calm Is. . .
- [ ] Never Alone
- [ ] Guard Your Treasure
- [ ] Never Judge
- [ ] I love Hugs
- [ ] What's the Plan?
- [ ] Pray, Pray, Pray. . .
- [ ] Sorrow to Joy
- [ ] Look!
- [ ] Safety and Security
- [ ] Winners
- [ ] Just for You
- [ ] What's Mine Is Yours
- [ ] No Buildup
- [ ] Give with a Big Heart
- [ ] Mission Impossible?
- [ ] Time to Grow
- [ ] Roots and Shoots
- [ ] Do You Love Me?
- [ ] Forget Regret
- [ ] The Look of Love
- [ ] Prayer Is. . .

June

- [ ] Hero Worship
- [ ] Who's Who?
- [ ] Thank You
- [ ] Here, There, and Everywhere
- [ ] Sleep Well
- [ ] More Than You Need
- [ ] On Your Marks. . .
- [ ] Get Set. . .
- [ ] Go!
- [ ] Treasure in Heaven
- [ ] Peace
- [ ] House on a Rock
- [ ] What to Do?
- [ ] Face Today with Me
- [ ] Around the Corner. . .
- [ ] Let's Talk
- [ ] "Jesus!"
- [ ] Wait for Me!
- [ ] Keep Going
- [ ] Safe and Secure
- [ ] Storms
- [ ] No Way Out
- [ ] Need Recharging?
- [ ] A Gentle Nudge
- [ ] Your Sunny Friend
- [ ] Slow Down
- [ ] Don't Stay Down
- [ ] Celebration
- [ ] Tomorrow Is Mine
- [ ] Pass It On

Contents *continued*

 If a subject or day was particularly special for you, mark the box as a reminder.

October

- [ ] Ask, Ask, Ask
- [ ] Lead On
- [ ] Peace
- [ ] True Beauty
- [ ] Divine Appointments
- [ ] Simple Trust
- [ ] Hidden Strength
- [ ] Look at Me
- [ ] Love
- [ ] Trust
- [ ] Praise First
- [ ] Greatest Gift?
- [ ] Steps of Faith
- [ ] No Going Back
- [ ] Immeasurable Wealth
- [ ] Praise!
- [ ] A Good Example
- [ ] Loneliness
- [ ] Hear My Answer
- [ ] You're Never Too Young
- [ ] A Special Guest
- [ ] A Warm Heart
- [ ] Faith
- [ ] Being Different
- [ ] No Time to Waste!
- [ ] Love Hurts Sometimes
- [ ] Do Your Best
- [ ] A Nice Surprise
- [ ] Well Done!
- [ ] Patience
- [ ] Dear You. . .

November

- [ ] Simple Prayer
- [ ] Let It Flow
- [ ] Make My Day
- [ ] "Jesus"
- [ ] Unfinished Business
- [ ] Something Good?
- [ ] Showing You Care
- [ ] Forgiven!
- [ ] Making Friends
- [ ] Something New
- [ ] The Big Picture
- [ ] No Words, Just Me
- [ ] Come to Me
- [ ] Follow the Instructions
- [ ] The Same Jesus
- [ ] One, Two, Then Three
- [ ] Small Things
- [ ] Let It Shine
- [ ] The Source of All Blessing
- [ ] Questions
- [ ] Smile!
- [ ] Love Is More
- [ ] It's Not Fair!
- [ ] Learn to Serve
- [ ] Knock, Knock
- [ ] The Real Me
- [ ] Love Is the Key
- [ ] Unhelpful Things
- [ ] Yes!
- [ ] Feeling Guilty

December

- [ ] Marks Out of Ten
- [ ] I Am. . .
- [ ] Stay Cool
- [ ] Oh, Dear
- [ ] What to Give?
- [ ] Expect Temptation
- [ ] Spiritual Growth
- [ ] My Kingdom
- [ ] Me First?
- [ ] Practice What I Preach
- [ ] The Gift of Today
- [ ] No Fear
- [ ] Relax and Enjoy!
- [ ] Storms
- [ ] Hidden in the Shadows
- [ ] Joy Is. . .
- [ ] Simply for You
- [ ] Now, Today!
- [ ] Guard Your Heart
- [ ] Is There No Hope?
- [ ] Large and Small
- [ ] I'm the Biggest
- [ ] Peacemaker
- [ ] Small Beginnings
- [ ] Happy Birthday
- [ ] The Gift Goes On
- [ ] Stay on Track
- [ ] Fact or Feeling
- [ ] Prayer Works
- [ ] Something for Everyone
- [ ] Jesus Is Everything!

My Special Promises to You

God is not like men, who lie; he is not a human who changes his mind. Whatever he promises, he does; he speaks, and it is done. Numbers 23:19 (GNB)

Answer to prayer

Even before they finish praying to me, I will answer their prayers.
Isaiah 65:24 (GNB)

Eternal life

For God loved the world so much that he gave his only Son, so that everyone who believes in him may not die but have eternal life.
John 3:16 (GNB)

Forgiveness

If we confess our sins to God, he will keep his promise and do what is right: he will forgive us our sins and purify us from all our wrongdoing.
1 John 1:9 (GNB)

Friendship

I do not call you servants any longer, because a servant does not know what his master is doing. Instead, I call you friends, because I have told you everything I heard from my father.
John 15:15 (GNB)

Guidance

Remember the Lord in everything you do, and he will show you the right way.
Proverbs 3:6 (GNB)

Joy

You will show me the path that leads to life; your presence fills me with joy and brings me pleasure forever.
Psalm 16:11 (GNB)

Love

But God has shown us how much he loves us— it was while we were still sinners that Christ died for us!
Romans 5:8 (GNB)

Peace

Peace is what I leave with you; it is my own peace that I give you. I do mot give it as the world does. Do not be worried and upset; do not be afraid.
John 14:27 (GNB)

Protection

But the Lord is faithful, and he will strengthen you and keep you safe from the Evil One.
2 Thessalonians 3:3 (GNB)

Rest

Come to me, all of you who are tired from carrying heavy loads, and I will give you rest.
Matthew 11:28 (GNB)

Reward

To those who win the victory I will give the right to sit beside me on my throne, just as I have been victorious and now sit by my Father on his throne.
Revelation 3:21 (GNB)

Victory

I have the strength to face all conditions by the power that Christ gives me.
Philippians 4:13 (GNB)

My Help When You Are. . .

Every one of you knows in his heart and soul that the LORD your God has given you all the good things that he promised. Every promise he made has been kept; not one has failed. Joshua 23:14 (GNB)

Anxious

Don't worry about anything, but in all your prayers ask God for what you need, always asking him with a thankful heart. And God's peace, which is far beyond human understanding, will keep your hearts and minds safe in union with Christ Jesus.
Philippians 4:7–7 (GNB)

Afraid

I am the Lord your God; I strengthen you and tell you, "Do not be afraid; I will help you."
Isaiah 41:13 (GNB)

Angry

Get rid of all bitterness, passion, and anger. No more shouting or insults, no more hateful feelings of any sort. Instead, be kind and tender-hearted to one another, and forgive one other, as God has forgiven you through Christ.
Ephesians 4:31–32 (GNB)

Feeling guilty

If we confess our sins to God, he will keep his promise and do what is right: he will forgive us our sins and purify us from all our wrongdoing.
1 John 1:9 (GNB)

In trouble

The good man suffers many troubles, but the LORD saves him from them all.
Psalm 34:19 (GNB)

In need	*And with all his abundant wealth through Christ Jesus, my God will supply all your needs.* Philippians 4:19 (GNB)
Lonely	*For God has said, "I will never leave you; I will never abandon you."* Hebrews 13:5 (GNB)
Sick	*"I will go and make him well," Jesus said.* Matthew 8:7 (GNB)
Tempted	*Every test that you have experienced is the kind that normally comes to people. But God keeps his promise, and he will not allow you to be tested beyond your power to remain firm; at the time you are put to the test, he will give you the strength to endure it, and so provide you with a way out.* 1 Corinthians 10:13 (GNB)
Tired	*He strengthens those who are weak and tired. Even those who are young grow weak; young men can fall exhausted. But those who trust in the LORD for help will find their strength renewed. They will rise on wings like eagles; they will run and not get weary; they will walk and not grow weak.* Isaiah 40:29–31 (GNB)

Books of the Bible

The Bible is a collection of books, like a library, and it is organized into two sections. The first section is the Old Testament, and the second is the New Testament.

Old Testament

Genesis	2 Chronicles	Daniel
Exodus	Ezra	Hosea
Leviticus	Nehemiah	Joel
Numbers	Esther	Amos
Deuteronomy	Job	Obadiah
Joshua	Psalms	Jonah
Judges	Proverbs	Micah
Ruth	Ecclesiastes	Nahum
1 Samuel	Song of Songs	Habakkuk
2 Samuel	Isaiah	Zephaniah
1 Kings	Jeremiah	Haggai
2 Kings	Lamentations	Zechariah
1 Chronicles	Ezekiel	Malachi

New Testament

Matthew
Mark
Luke
John
Acts
Romans
1 Corinthians
2 Corinthians
Galatians
Ephesians
Philippians
Colossians
1 Thessalonians
2 Thessalonians
1 Timothy
2 Timothy
Titus
Philemon
Hebrews
James
1 Peter
2 Peter
1 John
2 John
3 John
Jude
Revelation

How to Find a Bible Reference

A Bible reference is one word and two numbers, like this: John 3:16.

The word is the NAME of the book in the Bible. Names of books are written at the top of each page in your Bible. Use the index at the front to find where the book starts.

The first number is the CHAPTER, like the chapters of any book. These are the large numbers on the pages of your Bible.

The second number is the VERSE. Each chapter is split into small sections called verses. These are the small numbers on the pages of your Bible. The reference starts after the verse number.

Notes

Notes